MAXWELL'S RANCHE

Territory of New Mexico

Andrew J. Wahll
Curator, Aztec Mill
Cimarron, New Mexico

HERITAGE BOOKS
2013

HERITAGE BOOKS
AN IMPRINT OF HERITAGE BOOKS, INC.

Books, CDs, and more—Worldwide

For our listing of thousands of titles see our website
at
www.HeritageBooks.com

Published 2013 by
HERITAGE BOOKS, INC.
Publishing Division
5810 Ruatan Street
Berwyn Heights, Md. 20740

Copyright © 2013 Andrew J. Wahll

Heritage Books by the author:

Braddock Road Chronicles, 1755: From the Diaries and Records of Members of the Braddock Expedition and Others Arranged in a Day by Day Chronology

*Henry Mowat: Voyage of the Canceaux 1764–1776
Abridged Logs of H. M. Armed Ship Canceaux*

Sabino, Popham Colony (Maine) Reader: 1602–2003

Sea Raptors: Logs of Voyages of Private Armed Vessels, Comet and Chasseur, Commanded by Tom Boyle, 1812–1815

Westing: Personal Narratives of Life on the Rayado, New Mexico Frontier

Cover photograph courtesy of DeGolyer Library,
Southern Methodist University, Dallas Texas, Ag1999.1282.

All rights reserved. No part of this book may be reproduced or transmitted in any form or by any means, electronic or mechanical, including photocopying, recording or by any information storage and retrieval system without written permission from the author, except for the inclusion of brief quotations in a review.

International Standard Book Numbers
Paperbound: 978-0-7884-5483-7
Clothbound: 978-0-7884-6858-2

Table of Contents
1. Preface 4
2. Acknowledgements 5
3. Introduction 6
4. Source 7
5. Kaskaskia, Illinois 12
6. Aztec Mill Rock 14
7. Local building Activity 16
8. Quarry 17
9. Working and finishing 18
10. Tool Descriptions 20
11. Stone Walls 21
12. Maxwell's Ranche Comments 22
13. Illustrations 28
14. Cimarron Agency Letters 30
15. Bibliography 53

1. Preface
Maxwell's Ranche

The settlement here had been in the mind of Maxwell as early as 1858 when he returned to Kaskaskia, Illinois for the purpose to select household items for his mansion under construction. In 1861 he began construction of his Aztec Mill and the locale was to become known as Cimarron when the United States government established a post office by that name at Maxwell's Ranche with Lucien as postmaster. Whether the mill at any time was the site of the Post Office is not clear.

The written record of Cimarron Agency is included under the heading of LETTERS that come from U.S. Department of the Interior, Office of Indian Affairs. Records, New Mexico Superintendency. RG 75, National Archives, Washington, D.C. The Cimarron Agency was established in 1862 with responsibility for the Moache Ute and the Jicarilla Apache in northwestern New Mexico. Its forerunner was the Abiquiu Agency and the Utah Agency. The Cimarron Agency was consolidated with the Pueblo Agency in 1876 and the agency was discontinued and the Jicarilla Apaches were assigned to that agency, which was renamed the Jicarilla Agency in 1881. The supervision of the Jicarilla Agency was transferred to the Mescalero Agency in southern New Mexico in 1882. Many of these records are available on microfilm and are housed in the National Archives Rocky Mountain Region (Denver), Colorado, under the title of Cimarron Indian Agency (New Mexico), established in 1862. The author found, however, many of the original documents on microfilm are of poor quality and are difficult to read, those are indicated with dashes ---. Additionally, penmanship of many documents is difficult to read and I have tried herewith to include all of them.

Some of the letters of 1866 mention Maxwell's Ranche and are therefore a fitting opening to this book.

2. Acknowledgements
    Linda Davis: President Cimarron Historical Society and CS Cattle Company
    William and Catherine Hickman,
    Alfred (Buster) Chavez,
    Tim Farmer
    Jim Hollis,
    Charlotte Hollis,
    Bill Doer,
    Gene Lamm,
    Leslie Wolfinger,
    Debbie Riley,
    Pamalla Anderson, Head of Public Services, SMU who requested that the cover photo credit read:

DeGolyer Library, Southern Methodist University, Dallas Texas, Ag1999.1282.

3. Introduction

On searching the internet I casually entered into my search engine the phrase "Maxwell's Ranche" a term I encountered in my research on the Indian Agency for the Jicarilla and Ute Indians located in Cimarron, New Mexico. I was greatly surprised when the image popped up on my screen. Seeing this historic image changed completely my book concept. For the first time I could see new aspects of this 1860s Territory of New Mexico frontier settlement that became Cimarron including houses, mountain branch of the Santa Fe Trail, bridges, fence lines. The photograph captured a moment in time 152 years ago that will convey to the 2,000 plus mill visitors of today what Maxwell's Ranche was like back then.

4. Source:
Master of the Cimarron: Lucien B. Maxwell
By Lawrence R. Murphy New Mexico Historical Review, Vol. 55, No. 1, January, 1980, pp. 5-23.

In an article by Lawrence R. Murphy published in New Mexico Historical Review entitled "Master of the Cimarron: Lucien B. Maxwell (1980), Lawrence Murphy describes aspects of Maxwell's Ranche that are visible in the MSU Maxwell's Ranche photograph.

"Few nineteenth century New Mexicans achieved the lasting renown of Cimarron rancher Lucien B. Maxwell. (1) As owner of one of the largest and most hotly disputed Mexican land grants in the Southwest, he controlled vast properties in the northeastern section of the territory and southern Colorado. The location of an Indian agency at his ranch provided his with an assured market for agricultural produce, increased his wealth, and gave him considerable influence in Indian policy decisions. With the discovery of gold on the slopes of nearby Baldy Mountain, Maxwell's ranch became the center of a short-lasted rush of prospectors into the Sangre de Cristos, and Maxwell himself controlled mines which made him extremely rich. Most of all, however, what made Maxwell famous were his extensive Cimarron mansion, his renowned hospitality to visitors and his colorful personality. It is these aspects of his varied career upon which this article focuses.

Nearly twenty years of frontier experience preceded Maxwell's arrival on the Cimarron. Born in Kaskaskia, Illinois, September 14, 1818, he was the son of an Irish-born store keeper, his mother was the daughter of Pierre Menard, a highly successful trader and first Lieutenant Governor of Illinois. Lucien probably headed west soon after the death of his father (Hugh Maxwell) in an 1833 cholera epidemic, and by the mid-1830s was working for Bent, St. Vrain, and company in their trading posts along the South Platte and the Arkansas. In the years that followed, he became close friends with Kit Carson, accompanied John C. Fremont on two of his western expeditions, and, most important, married Luz Beaubien, whose Canadian-born father, Charles, had become one of the leading merchants in Taos and co-owner of a Mexican land grant on the eastern side of the Sangre de Cristo

Mountains. Following the death of Beaubien's son (Narcisco) in the Taos revolt, Maxwell moved to the banks of the Rayado, where he established on behalf of his father-in-law the first permanent settlement in that part of New Mexico.

By the mid-1850s Maxwell was ready to move. For close to two decades he had served apprenticeship on the frontier, learning important skills from the likes of Fremont, Carson, and Beaubien. He had come west as a poor teenager and adroitly accumulated the profits of several successful business ventures. Rayado, he recognized, was no place to build his empire. The settlement had been founded under Beaubien's auspices, and whoever lived there would inevitably fall under his shadow. Moreover, once the danger of Indian attack subsided, wagon trains often cut directly across the plains, east of what became known as Kit Carson Mesa, missing Rayado entirely. An old trail across the mountains to Taos fell into disuse as other more direct routes developed. And perhaps then as is occasionally still the case. A drought revealed how fickle a stream the Rayado could be; without water, crops died, and livestock has to be sold.

The banks of the Cimarron River, ten miles to the north of Rayado, offered much better possibilities. It was a larger and stronger stream, better fed and more reliable. The Cimarron poured out of the mountains through a narrow, picturesque canyon on to a broad, fertile plain, protected from winter storms by the low surrounding low hills. Here was ample room for thousands of sheep and cattle to graze and for vast fields of corn, wheat, and hay to grow. The Jicarilla Apache, who had once camped along its banks, were largely gone, and, as Surveyor John G. Parke had noted, the area had many strategic advantages in case of attack by the Plains Indians. Stages running between the eastern settlements and New Mexico often stopped here for night, and the Cimarron River had cut a fairly direct-although as yet largely undeveloped-route toward Taos. With sufficient energy and capital, the area could be developed into an important crossroads on northern New Mexico.

Exactly when Maxwell moved his headquarters to the Cimarron is uncertain. Farmers had lived there at least seasonally since the mid-1840s, and at first the Cimarron must have been one of several locations where herders watched Maxwell's herds of cattle and sheep. Probably by the mid-1850s, some of the Mexican-Americans who had farmed at Rayado moved there and began building a substantial residence and other buildings for

Maxwell. According to family tradition, Lucien talked about his plans for the Cimarron place during an 1858 visit to Kaskaskia. One of his objectives in making the long trip home may well have been to purchase furniture and other goods for the new house, and probably by 1857 or 1858, he has established himself and his family at what became known as "Maxwell's Ranche"

The house which Lucien built on the Cimarron quickly became one of the best-known landmarks in northern New Mexico. One visitor characterized it as a "palace when compared to the prevailing style of architecture in that country." "Palatial for that region," observed another, while a third termed it "exceedingly comfortable." In many ways the general design of the house was reminiscent of styles prevalent at Kaskaskia when Lucien was growing up there and in particular of his grandfather Menard's spacious residence overlooking the Mississippi. "It was built like a French villa," recalled British traveler William A. Bell, "with an open court inside and a verandah, running the whole length of the building, covered by a projecting roof." There were dormered windows on the second floor, and massive brick chimneys rising above a peaked roof. Like early all houses in New Mexico, the edifice was built of sun-dried adobe brick, although Lucien had white-washed the structure to give it the "appearance of a modern brick building." "It was large and roomy," recalled Colonel Henry J. Inman, a frequent visitor, "purely American in its construction."

The inside of the house, too, impressed visitors. The rooms were large," remembered Irving Howbert, having high ceilings finished with molding." The main dining room, where Maxwell entertained his male visitors, was "an extended rectangular affair," which in Inman's opinion "might properly have been termed the Baronial Hall... There," he reported, "Maxwell received his friends, transacted business with his vassals, and held high carnival at times." A separate dining room and parlor were provided for the women, in accordance with accepted New Mexico custom, and there were numerous sleeping rooms upstairs and down for family members, guests, and servants.

At first, perhaps before he had an opportunity to make buying trips east or to accumulate enough money to pay for expensive furnishings many of the rooms were empty of furniture. The room Irving Howbert slept in "was carpeted but had not even a chair. " In one corner stood a pile of wool mattresses and bedding which servants made into a bed at night. "So far as we saw," he went on, "there was only one room in the house that had a bedstead, and that was the one occupied by Maxwell and his wife." "I have slept on its hardwood floor," Henry Inman reminisced with the pride of one who had partaken in history, "rolled up in my blanket."…The house was only one of several structures Maxwell had built on the south bank of the Cimarron. There was a large wooden barn which reminded one visitor of many he had observed in Pennsylvania. The structure may not have been entirely suited to New Mexico, for one of the Indian agents assigned to Cimarron complained of having to store his annuity goods there, mixed up with Lucian's "produce and dye stuffs," because they were subject to the destructive powers of "hundreds of industrious mice." In another smaller building two Navajo women spent their days weaving rugs on Indian style looms. Nearby was a general store, "well filled with everything necessary for a frontier man's life," supplying goods to local residents and serving as a wholesaler to a number of smaller stores in the region. The business must have been one of Lucien's more profitable activities, for, as William Hoehne, who did business there for many years, reported, a three to five hundred percent markup on merchandise was common….Maxwell's most ambitious building project was a massive stone mill for grinding (cutting) corn and wheat into flour (meal). Alone among his major buildings, it has survived well over a hundred years and serves as a museum dedicated to preserving historic relics of the area. To supervise its erection, Maxwell had already hired by 1860 a Boston-born engineer, B.M. Blackmore, a millwright Emory Williams, a New Yorker, and a Vermont-born mason, James Truax. The work must have gone slowly, for in mid-summer 1864, The Santa Fe New Mexican reported that Maxwell, whom the editor described as "one of our most prominent and successful stockmen, "was building a 'grist mill' capable of turning out three hundred barrels of flour per day." The editor added that he welcomed "all such enterprises as indications of the onward progress of our territory." Two years later (1866), a visitor found the "lately finished" mill to be "well and complete (sic) constructed and the machinery perfect." The excellence of the flour which he saw attested to the general success of the undertaking.

    The mill, too, turned a handsome profit for Maxwell. In addition to supplying food for the Indian agency which was located at the ranch after 1861, Maxwell found ready markets for corn meal and wheat flour among the growing towns of New Mexico and Colorado and sold substantial quantities to the military headquarters at Fort Union. During the Civil War, when New Mexico was cut off for many months from trade to the south, there was a greater demand for grain, wheat, and oats than could be supplied, and prices were correspondingly inflated. As a result, as John D. Lee reported, once the mill was complete, it kept grinding "most all the time" just to keep up with the increasing demand. The mill also played an important role in the personal life of Maxwell, for it was there (on the third floor) where his eldest daughter Virginia secretly married Indian agent A.S.B. Keyes, and enraged her disapproving father (Lucian Bonaparte Maxwell).

    The importance of the Maxwell ranch received official recognition in 1861 when the United States government established a post office at what was now to be known as Cimarron. The first postmaster, not surprisingly, was Lucien Maxwell. That same year Maxwell's Ranche became a stop on the newly established Missouri Stage Company line connecting Kansas City with Santa Fe, and in 1868 the opening of a telegraph office at Lucien's connected Cimarron directly with the East.

5. Kaskaskia, Illinois

Lucien Maxwell grew up in Kaskaskia, Illinois which was then on a small peninsula that jutted out in to the Mississippi River just north of the present-day location of Chester, Illinois. The peninsula is now an island, cut off from the state by a channel change in the Mississippi River that took place decades ago and can only reached from Missouri by a bridge between Ste Genevieve and St. Mary's which crosses the Mississippi River. The early town was founded by French settlers and Jesuit missionaries and the congregation built its first stone church in 1714. A trading post for the fur trade at the village became a meeting place for the whole territory and was a jumping off place for explorations to the west. From the French, the Indians, and the mixed-race descendants became voyagers and coureur de bois with all the prairie tribes and beyond with the Spanish colony in New Mexico. The French were in control in 1740s building agriculture settlements in the Illinois Country that were important for supplying Lower Louisiana especially New Orleans, with wheat and corn. Farmers shipped tons of flour south over the years, as those staple crops could not be grown in Louisiana's climate. As the area grew, in 1804, Kaskaskia became a land-office town and the territorial capitol in 1809. The town was made of stone mansions and homes of typical French architecture building types brought up from New Orleans. Louisiana. New Orleans consumed great quantities of wheat and corn shipping tons of flour over the years, as those staple crops could not be grown in Louisiana's climate. Typical of the French Colonial architecture the Mid-Mississippi River Valley is the Pierre Menard house near Kaskaskia , called "the Mount Vernon of the West", built in the early 1800's It is a low and broad, of one story and the roof sweeping out over a columned porch "galerie" the entire length of the house. Menard was the grandfather of Lucien Bonaparte Maxwell and Lucien must have known the house in detail and it served as a model for Maxwell's Cimarron house. The Pierre Menard house built in 1802, was a place famous throughout the West for its hospitality much as did "Maxwell's Ranche" sixty years later and half a continent away. Another house located in Prairie du Rocher, is Creole House built in 1800 and rebuilt in the 1960s. Creole House had many architectural similarities to Maxwell's Ranche house. The oldest structure in the Midwest is the Fort de Charters powder magazine that has survived from the French period, this massive barrel vaulted masonry building now with a peaked roof has been restored and reconstructed for the visitor of today. Another large masonry building that Lucien must have known as a youth was the main gate of Fort de Chartes. A map of Kaskaskia drawn in 1766 by Thomas Hutchins shows town roads, buildings framed by the Mississippi and Kaskaskia Rivers . Another map gives us more associations of Lucien to Kaskaskia. A map by Thomas Hutchins drawn in 1771 shows two water powered mills, and a wind driven grist mill nearby. During the colonial era , bateaux and pirogues (water craft of the period) loaded with barrels of flour descended the Mississippi from Kaskaskia to supply New Orleans. These mills were important supplying residents of New Orleans with the essential ingredient for their baguettes and beignets, without which life in Illinois Country would have faltered .

6. Aztec Mill Rock

In the collection of the Aztec Mill is a framed map mounted on the wall entitled "Colfax County 1876". This map with a detailed legend shows land use, physical features, roads and cattle trails. What is significant about the map is a prominent road running north from Cimarron to Chase Ranch. This road could possibly show the route used to move the sandstone south from quarry to mill site. Additionally displayed is a photo of Aztec mill masonry blocks a detail that shows the precision of the mason's skills.

Sandstone (arenite) is a sedimentary rock composed mainly of sand-sized minerals and rock grains. Most sandstone is composed of quartz and/or feldspar as these are the most common minerals in the Earth's crust. Sandstone is mined by quarrying and is used for domestic construction and house wares. Sandstone has been a popular building material from ancient times. It is relatively soft, making it easy to carve. The formation of sandstone involves two principal stages. First, a layer or layers of sand accumulates as the result of sedimentation, either from water or from air. Once it has accumulated, the sand becomes sandstone when it is compacted by pressure of overlying deposits and cemented by the precipitation of minerals within the pore spaces between the sand grains.

The report entitled "Chase Orchard: A Poñil Phase Pueblo in the Northeastern New Mexico" by James A. Gunnerson speaks to the significant features of the region including the Cimarron Crescent, a large archaeological and resource region between Moreno Valley and Canadian River and the "Old North Trail" which was the ancient route along the shoulder of the Rocky Mountains following the foothills of the Rockies from Canada to Mexico.

Gunnerson has the following description of the location of the source of sandstone used in construction of Aztec Milll: "Site Setting - Chase Orchard Pueblo is located near the middle of the lower Poñil Canyon some five miles in length, this lower section extends from the canyon's mouth to where Chase Canyon enters from the north. With the five mile span of this lower section of the canyon floor drops nearly 200 feet in elevation, although one senses little elevation change driving along the canyon. Near the mouth of Chase Canyon the Poñil's valley floor is almost non-existent, but at Poñil Canyon's mouth the valley is nearly a mile wide. This width is a little deceptive because it is enhanced by its merging with the bottomlands along the Cimarron River. Throughout its length, the left (or north) wall of the Poñil Canyon is striking, rising over a thousand feet above the canyon floor. A bluff forming the prominent landmark known as Indian Head lies at the east end of Poñil Canyon's mouth and juts almost 1200 feet above the plains to the east. Although the right (south) wall is of comparable height, erosion has receded it farther away and dissected it with several lesser canyons.

The bedrock exposed along the lower Poñil Canyon is composed primarily of Tertiary sandstones (Poison Canyon and Raton formations) and Cretaceous sandstones (Vermejo and Trinidad formation; Robinson et al. 1962: Plate 3). The lower slopes of the canyon are Pierre Shale, the weathering of which has contributed to the fine textures of soils and sediments common along Poñil Creek. Capping the uplands adjacent Poñil Creek and its three forks are Tertiary sandstones and conglomerates (Ibid.). Erosion of these uplands adds some sand and gravel to sediments washed down the Poñil drainage."

7. Local building activity (Fort Union)

As Fort Union was under construction at the same time as the mill, there were many men with masonry skills living and working in the area. "Fort Union NM: Fort Union and the Frontier Army in the Southwest - Historic Resource Study" provides background to events in the area that included Maxwell's Ranch. "In the spring of 1865 Chief Quartermaster McFerran was unable to hire the necessary skilled workers within the military department to fill the jobs available on the buildings being erected at the Fort Union Depot. He requested that a number of craftsmen, including carpenters, tinners, and plasterers be sent from Fort Leavenworth to do the job, with the army providing transportation and an attractive salary ($85 per month, compared to the $65 paid to artisans already on the job). In addition, enlisted men who possessed the necessary skills were released from military duty and employed to work on the depot. While so engaged they received the same wages as civilian employees instead of their military pay. Soon after craftsmen arrived from Fort Leavenworth in September 1865, the employees already on the job objected to the gap between their pay and that of the new workers. The issue was resolved by raising their pay to the same level. Table 9 Civilian Employees Authorized at Fort Union Depot, 1867 lists the following masonry trades and the number of men involved:

>   Quarrymen   6
>   Stone masons 10
>   Chief mason   1
>   Masons   24

It could be that Maxwell had difficulty in keeping working crews at Aztec Mill due to higher wages paid at Fort Union this being the cause.

8. Quarry A block was broken away from its bed by a row of wedges. Wooden wedges were driven in tight and then wetted to make them expand, or metal wedges were driven in with a sledgehammer. Several hours after wetting the wood the wedges expanded just enough to split loose the blocks. To avoid hauling extra weight, blocks were cut to the appropriate shape and size for the building before being taken from the quarry by wagon. Quarriers had to be careful to use sound rock even though it was more difficult to work. Blasting was not extensively used because surface rock was easily accessible from the formation. By the middle of the 18th century drills or jumpers were employed for cutting holes in blocks. The drill is a long piece of iron with a chisel-like end; it was struck with a sledgehammer by one workman and held by another, who rotated it after each blow. Smaller drills could be operated by one workman.

9. Working and Finishing Rock

American stoneworkers were distinguished according to their tasks: Quarriers extracted and roughly shaped the blocks; rough-masons "dressed" or finished blocks and cut straight moldings; freemasons carved the more intricate shapes and cut curved moldings. All specialists had laborers to assist them. A master-mason directed the stonework. He checked it for accuracy, made templates and drew details when needed and not provided by the architect. A stoneworker learned his craft under the direction of a master, to whom he was apprenticed for a term of three to seven years.

There were five basic methods of stone dressing that include 1) hewing with ax or pick, 2) hammering with an ax or hammer, 3) working with a chisel by a mallet, 4) sawing and rubbing with an abrasive. The use of chisels required more skills than the use of the ax. With hammer and pounding stone, the first step in squaring a block was to banker up (placement on masons work bench) the widest bed or surface. The workman drew a straight line at one edge and then pitched or spalled off debris or waste above it; a pitching chisel was the tool used for the purpose. This first draft was then refined with a cutting chisel or ax. Next, a draft was made on an adjoining edge of the surface, perpendicular to the first one, and verified with a square. These two drafts defined the plane of the finished surface. By careful use of straightedges and by sighting, the remaining two drafts were cut. The rest of the surface was then reduced to the degree of uniformity desired, with a point, hammers, chisels or a combination of tools. The surface just completed became the bottom bed of the stone. Then the face of the stone was dressed. After that the top bed was finished, then the end joints and finally the inner joint or surface. The color rubbed off onto the high points and indicated to the workman the areas that needed to be further reduced.

Several tools were used in sequence to finish a stone. The work could be terminated as any stage that corresponded to the desired degree of finish. The nature and hardness of the material determined what tools were employed, although there was some freedom of choice. Working and finishing different typed of stone had the following steps: 1) Split with drill holes and wedges and/or "scabble" with a pick (at the quarry). 2a) Establish corners with a pitching chisel and/or 2b) "Draft" the margins with a tooth chisel 3) Bring the surface to a rough finish with a tooth chisel. 4) Cut off the ridges with a wide chisel (called "tool"); the grooves made by the tooth chisel usually show to some extent. 5) If desired, the surface can be rubbed smooth with an abrasive.

Each tool had a specific function and method of application. The marks left on the surface of a stone by the last tool used, or the last two tools, can frequently be distinguished if the material is not too weathered. Many of the blocks seen in Aztec Mill exhibit these markings.

10. Tool descriptions

Sledgehammers weighed from 10 to 25 pounds. They had two square faces and a long handle; they were intended to be held by the workman with both hands and were swung with considerable force. They were primarily employed at the quarry, for driving drills and wedges, knocking off rough projections and breaking rock.

Drills or jumpers were round, hexagonal or octagonal in section, up to three long, with a chisel-like or flattened point at one end. They were used to cut holes into rock at the quarry, to split off stones and to sub-divided large stones.

Wedges were of hard wood and copper from ancient times but iron or steel wedges have been more commonly used during the last five hundred years. Various tapered shapes have been employed in round holes a type of wedge called plug and feathers was used; a round tapered plug was driven between two hollow semicircular feathers placed in a hole. These were of various length and diameters.

Picks were the mason's pickax but shorter and stouter than those used for digging and pointed on both ends. It was used for rough dressing of sandstone and limestone at the quarry.

Points were round or octagonal in section about 12 inches long when new and sharpened to a pyramidal point. They were used on hard stones to remove material quickly. A point was held in one hand and struck with a hammer held in the workman's other hand; it had to be sharpened frequently and was discarded when worn down to a length of about five inches

Pitching Chisels (pitchers) were a heavy chisel, about one and one-eighth inches in diameter with a cutting edge of 2 and half inches. The cutting edge was not sharpened and the only use for pitching off the edges of a stone that was being squared up.

Chisels were used by early Egyptian stoneworkers made of stone, copper and bronze but the importance of the chisel as a tool for working stone emerged with iron and steel usage. The chisel was held in one hand, at an angle of about 35 degrees to the plane of the stone. The chisel was tapped with a wooden mallet or iron hammer, whose weight varied with the softness or hardness of the stone, Stones were usually cut before the ground water in them, called quarry sap, had dried out. In this condition they were softer and easier to work with a chisel or other tools.

11. Stone Walls

Masonry work on buildings must begin with hoisting stones too heavy to be lifted into position by hand. These were hoisted up using rope and pulley or pulled by hand on ramps supported by scaffolding. (Figure 26)

Most stone buildings depended on mortar between the individual stones. Attention had to be given to selecting and layering stones so as to bond or interweave them, in order to make the wall strong. Bonding is most apparent on the exterior face of the wall but the stones on the interior of a wall were also be bonded by mortar.

Working and Finishing Lifting and transporting;

Handling large stones, which weigh from 140 to 180 pounds per cubic foot, is difficult. The great masses of stone split off at the quarry were broken up on the spot, to the approximate size needed for the building. If the subdivided pieces were too heavy to be turned or lifted by a few men, levers were used or manipulate them onto a sled.

Stone was transported on sleds pulled by oxen during the winter. Winter was the best season for moving rock because animals were not needed for farm or ranch work, and with freezing temperatures, ice could be used to facilitate movement of stone pieces.

Working and Finishing Lifting and transporting.

Handling large stones, which weigh from 140 to 180 pounds per cubic foot, is difficult. The great masses of stone split off at the quarry were broken up on the spot, to the approximate size needed for the building. If the subdivided pieces were too heavy to be turned or lifted by a few men, levers were used or manipulate them onto a sled (stone boat).

Stone was transported on sleds pulled by oxen during the winter. Winter was the best season for moving rock because animals were not needed for farm or ranch work, and with freezing temperatures, ice could be used to facilitate movement of stone pieces.

12. Maxwell's Ranche Photograph Comments

According to the documentation prepared by Southern Methodist University, the photographic image is an albumen print that dates from ca. 1860-1867. The albumen silver print process was invented in 1850 by Louis Desire Blanquart-Evrard and was the first commercially available method of producing a photographic image on a paper base from a negative. It used the albumen found in egg whites to bind the photographic chemicals to the paper and became the dominant form of photographic positives from 1855 to 20th century with a peak in the 1860-90 period.

Albumen printing paper was the medium of choice for the majority of photographic printers for 30 years from when introduced in 1850s having fine detail and the greatest tonal range compared to other processes as well as the sharp definition of albumen paper to be ideal for architectural photography. Another photographic printing process was daguerreotype using a light sensitive silver or silver-covered copper plate to directly capture an image without a negative of the image. Louis Daguerre introduced his process in 1839.

Dating the of Maxwell's Ranche photo precisely is problematical as early structures in Cimarron having known dates of 1870 or earlier are not shown in the photo. These include National Hotel (1858), Schwenk's Hall (1864), Immaculate Conception Catholic Church (1864) and Barlow, Sanderson & Company Stage Office (1866) according to dates listed in "A Walking Tour of Old Town Cimarron, New Mexico in the 1800s". The following structures are visible in the photo: Dold Brothers Warehouse (1848), Maxwell's House (1858), Maxwell's Guest House (1858), Aztec Mill (1864), and Maxwell's Corral.
The St. James Hotel built in 1872, the center of old town Cimarron is not visible in the photo.

The photo shows Maxwell's Mansion and adjacent guest house. Maxwell's Mansion is surrounded by a decorative white fence with gate. The photo reflects closely the architectural model on exhibit at the entry way of Aztec Mill. The scale model of the mill was built by Roy Tozier in 1906 and is on display at Aztec Mill courtesy of Philmont Scout Ranch.

The details shown on the digital image from SMU are unique and after hours of study the following are my observations. In studying the digital image, the content becomes problematical with large magnification, definition is lost – examples of this include possibly two women (servants?) on the front steps of Maxwell's Mansion, a large black guard dog outside of Aztec Mill (Maxwell did have a kennel of hunting dogs). Another example of motion blurring is possibly four riders or more within the fence of Maxwell's wagon yard along with a light coach that possibly is a Dougherty Spring Wagon.

Adjacent to Maxwell's mansion is the elongated frame building described as being built by M.R. Whiteman as his house and a freight depot for the Andres Dawes stage line. The same building is shown on early maps as Dold Brothers Warehouse (1861) that Lucian Maxwell used a commissary, a freight depot, a trading post and Indian Agency. The decorative wooden eves of this building are visible and the building now has a brick veneer. The photo shows a road up from Cimarron River past a rather large fenced garden plot. The Cimarron River is visible as it meanders over the flood plain. The river channel over the flood plain is considerably different from today. This river channel is shown in the 1865 map of Cimarron that is published in Maria E Montoya's study "Translating Property the Maxwell Land Grant and the Conflict over Land in the American West, 1840-1900". This map shows the Cimarron as it was in 1865 and the photo reflects the Cimarron map. Maxwell's corral and stable is shown surrounded by earthen embankments. Outside the embankment is a large adobe structure with a large hay wagon nearby. Three dwellings are on the west edge of the photo along with ditch segments possibly being excavated for the headrace. The ditch to the mill appears in a map by the Cimarron Hydrographic Survey drawn in 1923 and it flows into the mill opening via a wooden sluice however the course of the river over a large area of the photo is not clear. The river flows over the flood plain from the mill via a channel called the tailrace that carries the spent water back to the Cimarron River not visible in the photo.

At the center of the scene are two simple wooden log bridges over the Cimarron, one below Maxwell's Corral this is the Mountain Branch of the Santa Fe Trail. The other bridge that appears to be higher and is partly hidden by vegetation this would connect the center of Old Town Cimarron to the Aztec Mill and Maxwell's Corral. Near this bridge is a large fenced and well maintained field probably a garden. The Beaubien and Maxwell Family Graves of 1864 are not visible being obscured by trees.

The Aztec Mill building in the photograph appears to be complete however there is nothing in the photo to indicate that the mill was in operation. Early on the mill was used as a storage facility for Maxwell's Indian Agency.

Beyond Maxwell's yard are well maintained fencing that surround three plowed plots that will become Cimarron and the site of St. James Hotel in 1872. In the background is a large wooden building having two peaks of two connected parts as well as smaller ancillary buildings, these are possibly precursor buildings of Maxwell Land Grant & Railway Company holdings built in 1874.

This is possibly the is the earliest photograph of Cimarron and based on the structures I would say it shows Cimarron of 1862, the key item is the presence of the mill however the building could have existed without having the grist mill functioning for at least two years. The tablet above the second floor door reads:

Aztic Mills
1864.

The spelling of Aztic is in error however the plural mills is correct as there were up to three stone sets each with a bed and runner stone on the first floor (the stone floor). Many have asked me why it was misspelled and I have to say that I have no idea why.

The vegetation of the surrounding hills is less than found today

When Lucian Maxwell decided to build a mill at his new settlement on the Cimarron River he had to overcome major obstacles stemming from the unique stone building he planned. As a youth he probably had visited the three mills in Kaskaskia, Illinois shown on a map prepared by Thomas Hutchins in 1771 entitled "A Plan of the several Villages in the Illinois Country with part of the River Mississippi." The Hutchins map shows the location of three grist mills (two waterpowered and one powered by the wind as well as the early location of Kaskaskia on a peninsula that juts into a bend of the Mississippi River.
A second Hutchins map drawn in 1764 entitled a "Plan of Caskaskies" has been adapted to show Kaskaskia town and is included in HISTORICAL ATLAS OF CANADA chapter titled "French Interior Settlements, 1750s." Atlas plate 41 shows the town plan along with the following note:

"With 350 people of French descent and 321 slaves Kaskaskia had about half of the non-native population of the Illinois settlements in 1752. Most buildings were of stone. The largest farmer had 200 hectares under cultivation...A few large landowners produced considerable surpluses, the Jesuit missionary at Kaskaskia estimated that the Illinois settlement raised three times what they consumed. Wheat and flour, corn, cattle and swine were shipped to Louisiana, often for Caribbean markets."

On the Cimarron River there was no suitable building stone nearby. This meant Lucian had to find a quarry site. There was a sandstone formation (along the Poñil River this was the Tertiary Sandstones (Poison Canyon and Raton formations) and Cretaceous sandstones. Capping the uplands adjacent to Poñil Creek and its three forks are Tertiary sandstones and conglomerates. Erosion of these uplands adds some sand and gravel to sediments washed down the Poñil drainage. As I surveyed the land forms with people knowledgeable about local quarries, one quarry site was apparent. Not having permission from Chase Ranch to trespass their property I did not examine any sites on their property, one site visible from NM Route 204 appears to have approach access and significant working surfaces these are shown in the attached photo collection.

I could visualize large sandstone pieces were broken loose from the formation and roughly dressed and then loaded on to a stone boat (simple sled) and latter on to quarry wagons pulled by oxen teams away from the quarry face and then down to the road on the valley floor. The route to the building site could follow the valley floor to the ancient route beneath Indian Hand and along the highlands toward the valley of the Cimarron River. Surveying other routes, the cross county route is shown on the modern topographic map. This route was shorter but had topographic issues that heavily loaded wagons had to overcome.

 The total drop in elevation from quarry to building site is 160 feet. The heavily loaded wagons dropped down toward the floodplain and crossed over the Cimarron flood plain to the far side of the flood plain approaching the steep river bank where the mill would be built. On the east edge of the flood plain there would be the massive foundation excavation,. Historically it was known that due to the vibration of the wood and or metal machinery, the foundation had to be deep and broad to minimize the effect of vibration. To accomplish this massive stones were placed well below grade. The foundation opening was dug by horse drawn scrapers, and crews wielding picks and shovels that removed surface soil down to bed rock. The scope of the excavation is hinted at in the cellar. The blocks were laid down closely and then fitted together by the mason and covered by mortar that held them together.

Stone masons visiting the Aztec Mill in 2012 have commented to the author on construction techniques: "With regard to the stone foundation, walls were first raised up from the corners of the building with the walls then being filled in from the four corners. To build the wall, wooden scaffolding made of lodgepole pine was lashed together for a framework". Walkways and masonry work areas made of wooden planks were also lashed together with rope. Rock was carried to the base of the building and there shaped roughly to fit into the wall rising above. These rock pieces were hoisted to the rock wall above by horse drawn rope block and tackle. At the rising wall the mason did final block shaping and placement. Working from the exterior frame work of poles and planks the timber scaffolding was secured to the building through window and door openings and lashed to the counterpart scaffolding on the interior of the building.

The dimensional stability was insured by the four S shaped fittings on the front and on the rear walls, the fittings were bolted to iron rods called tie rods that were attached to the main wooden beams with large lag bolts.(Figure 26)

These elements were created by local blacksmiths and positioned when the building was built in 1862. On front and back the S shaped fittings are secured by threaded ends that hold a large square nut that secured the eight (front and back) ornamental S fittings to the massive wooden beams that tied together the front and rear walls further stabilizing the entire mill. In the 1960's(?) steel cables were wrapped top to bottom, around the building to stabilize the mill side to side.

A photo of 1930 seems to show the results of a tremor that caused cracking in the front fabric of the mill which was subsequently pointed up over the entire building. Later steel cables are visible on the third floor providing support for the roof trusses.

The millrace to conveying water to operate the mill is not apparent in the photograph.

What is shown is that it is probably being planned or under construction on the back side of the building, In the photo

Cimarron River water flowed much closer to the mill than today, this is accurately shown on the Cimarron Map drawn in 1865. The author theorizes that spent water from the water wheel and the water wheel pool exited the mill through a tailrace possibly beneath the back door opening or the two adjacent openings (channels) adjacent to the back door (today these openings are partially bricked up with windows on the upper portioned. Archaeological excavation could easily verify if water exiting the waterwheel pool flowed beneath the floor to openings under mill the doorway or through companion openings now functioning as windows.

The detailed source map showing source of water had not yet been completed and is not shown in the Maxwell's Ranche photo. The photo predates the map drawn in 1923 where is shown the linear feature labeled "Old Mill Ditch" drawn for the Cimarron Hydrographic Survey. Photographs by the author document the head gate on the Cimarron located four miles above the mill site also shown is the iron pipe over an arroyo and a vehicular bridge for the same purpose.

Immaculate Conception Catholic Church is documented as being built in 1864. The building shown in the photograph is a later version of the 1864 church that exists today (see Walking tour of Old Town Cimarron) however it does not appear in the Maxwell's Ranche photograph nor is any construction activity apparent.

Double peaked building on left side of photo and adjacent building are possibly Maxwell Land Grant & Railway buildings. These are mentioned in "A Walking Tour of Old Town Cimarron, New Mexico in the 1800s"

All fencing in the photo appears to be well built and maintained. Near the mill it appears to be wire strung between wooden posts. Around Lucian's house it is a sturdy wooden white painted decorative ornamental fence. Around the plaza it is wire and in the foreground it is wooden rails between posts.

The photograph is a albumen print measuring 14 x 20 cm on 20 x 25.5 cm. mount which has a digitization date of 2012 and is displayed as .jp2; uploaded as .jpg. The archival scan was 6128 wide x 4932 high pixels, 48-bit RGB .

13. Illustrations

Follows last page of text

Figure 1 Portrait of Lucien Bonaparte Maxwell.

Figure 2 Map showing Illinois Country where Lucien grew up and Location of three grist mills drawn by Thomas Hutchins in 1771.

Figure 3 Map of Kaskaskia drawn by Thomas Hutchins in 1766 Shows town roads, buildings, Mississippi River and Kaskaskia River.

Figure 4 Summarized map of Illinois Country as printed in Historical Atlas of Canada, 1987 showing Roads, French settlement, Indian settlements, mills, rivers.

Figure 5 Map of Cimarron 1865 shows early buildings (Maxwell's Corral, Maxwell House, Store, Mill) and residences with cultivated plots and crops grown.

Figure 6 Pierre Menard House is a historic house once occupied by Lucien's grandfather. Built in early 1800s of vertical logs.

Figure 7 Creole House that is very similar to the house of Lucien Maxwell shown in Maxwell's Ranche photograph. House was built in 1801 and is located Prairie du Rocher, Illinois.

Figure 8 Masonry of Main gate at Fort de Chartes located at Kaskaskia.

Figure 9 Powder magazine begun in 1753 is oldest surviving non-Indian structure in Midwest. A masonry building in scope and size to Aztec Mill in Cimarron built by Lucien Maxwell..

Figure 10 Maxwell's Ranche photograph. This wide angle view is the earliest photo of settlement that would become Cimarron, NM and surrounding environs.

Figure 11 Close up view of Maxwell's Wagon yard showing Aztec Mill, Maxwell's houses, trading post/store and log structures.

Figure 12 Extreme close up view of Maxwell's Wagon yard showing: wagon, two log buildings, two sets of wagon wheels and reduced images of groups of mounted riders.

Figure 13 Doughtery Spring Wagon 1882

Figure 14 Satellite view of source of mill sandstone with transport routes to Cimarron.

Figure 15 View of location of quarry from NM route 204

Figure 16 Quarry site photograph taken from NM route 204

Figure 17 Close up of Quarry site work surfaces, photo taken from

NM route 204
Figure 18 Aztec Mill masonry detail showing sandstone blocks used in Mill construction
Figure 19 Cimarron River flood plain today, site of Maxwell's Corral
Figure 20 Source of mill water, map drawn by Cimarron Hydrographic Survey 1923
Figure 21 Building foundation as drawn by Oliver Evans, published in "TheYoung Mill-Wright and MillersGuide1798"
Figure 22 Construction scaffolding. The author points out this sketch of stone work, iron work and scaffolding is adapted to Aztec Mill, Cimarron, NM from a drawing in the "Mill" by David Macaulay, published by Houghton Mifflin Company of Boston, MA in 1983.
Figure 23 Mill masonry construction tools have changed little since the advent of steel.
Figure 24 Mill masonry construction tools
Figure 25 Mill masonry construction tools
Figure 26 Diagram: Bankering up a Block of Stone
Figure 27 Aztec Mill on ration day 1868.
Figure 28 Aztec Mill back view

14. Letters from Bureau of Indian Affairs and others
Cimarron Agency Letters

The below letters describe the problems, business and issues of Jicarilla and Ute peoples living in the Cimarron Agency in the northeast corner of the Territory of New Mexico. The three dashes symbol (---) indicate illegibility due to the period manuscript's age and grammer as written reflecting period usage.

Office Superintendent – Indian Affairs
Santa Fe, NM
Sept 7, 1867

Maj. E.B. Dennison
U. S. Indian Agent
Cimarron, N.M.

Sir:
    Your letter of the 4th just arrived just arrived, in reply I would state that if you have invoices or bills of lading of goods belonging to the Abiquiu Agency forward the same to this office – no goods must be staffed at the Cimarron except those belonging to your agency which are marked E.B. Dennison US Agt Apache & Ute Cimarron Agency New Mexico: Com G. Murfling, Atchison, Kansas and Com. Begy St. Louis, Mo.
    The balance of the goods for Abiquiu and Santa Fe must come here as required by the contract. You will therefore have nothing to do with other goods not belonging to your agency, and when the goods arrive, sign nothing until you examine and see that you have everything your bills call for.
    If Mr. .Maxwell can't get that building ready for you by the time the goods arrive, you are hereby authorized to rent a building at Riado at the rate of $200 per annum, reserving the right to evacuate the same whenever you please as the government may authorize the building of an agency within the next year.
Yours Respectfully
Maj. E. B. Dennison
 U.S. Indian Agent
Cimarron N.Mex.

(Note: This correspondence suggests that the mill at Maxwell's Ranche was not complete as of Sept 7, 1867 which is three years later than the completion date carved in stone tablet above front door of Aztec Mill that reads: 1864. I believe the Maxwell Ranche photo shows the completed building shell, it is probable there was much interior carpentry and machinery work yet to complete as well as extensive water course construction (millrace, water wheel, and tailrace) before any grain could be cut by the stones – the term grinding is not the appropriate term that the author learned attending conferences presented by Society for Preservation of Old Mills held at Bucks County, PA, Alexandria, VA and Raleigh, NC).

Office Superintendant Indian Affairs
Santa Fe New Mexico
Col. A.D. Henderson
Sir:
You will immediately notify all the Indians belonging to the Cimarron Agency that the annuity goods will be distributed at Mr. Maxwell's on 10th day of November next. I will be --- a few days before – Mr Labidi is here and will proceed immediately to receive yours. You will then return to Santa Fe.
I am Respectfully yours
    A. B. Norton
    Supr. Indian Affairs
    N. Mexico
Col. A. D. Henderson
U.S. Indian Agent
Cimarron, N.M.

Office Supt. Indian Affairs
Santa Fe New Mexico Dec 15th 1866
Hon L. V. Bogy

Sir:
I have the honor to report that during the month of November, the Indians of this Superintendency have been peaceable and well disposed towards the Government of the United States and but few if any depredations have been committed by them so far as this Department have been informed.
    On the third of the month, I left Santa Fe for the Cimarron Agency to distribute the annunity goods to the Utahs and Apaches of said Agency.
    The goods were distributed on the 8th and 9th – Major Dennison arrived in time to deliver the goods, take charge of them --- and assist in the distribution.
    The Indians appeared very much satisfied with the amount of goods presented, and demonstrated no hostile nor warlike intentions and I think will remain at peace at least during the winter.
    Business finished I returned to Santa Fe Leaving Maj. Dennison in full charge of his agency.
    With the exception of a few visits by Indians nothing more of interest worthy of note has transpired at this Superintendency during the month ending November 30th 1866.

Very Respectfully your obedient Servant.
A.B. Norton
Supt. Indian Affairs N. Mex.
M. Davis, Clerk

Office Supt. Indian Affairs
Santa Fe New Mexico Dec 16th 1866
Mr. L. Maxwell

Sir
    Herewith enclosed please find a copy of letter from this Department in reference to your elevation as U.S. Indian Agent for New Mexico.
Very Respectfully your ---
A.B. Norton Superintendent
Ind. Affairs N. Mex
N.M. --- Davis, Clerk

Mr. --- Maxwell, Esq.
Cimarron, New Mexico

Office Supt Indian Affairs
Santa Fe New Mexico Jan 12 1866
Hon. L. V. Bogy

Sir
    I have the honor to report that during the month ending December 31st 1866 the Indians under charge of this Superintendency have conducted themselves in a peaceable manner toward the Government and have committed but few if any depredations upon the citizens of this Territory at least none have been reported at this office.
    With the general number of visits made by small detachments of Indians nothing of interest to the department has transpired which should be reported.
Very Respectfully Your Obt. Servant
A. B. Norton
Supt Indian Affairs N. Mex
P. Mc. M Davis, Clerk

Hon. L.V. Bogy
---- Indian Affairs
Washington City D.C.
Office Suptr. of Ind. Affairs
Santa Fe N.M. Oct 25th 1870
John Collinson, Esq
President of the Maxwell Land Grant and Railroad Co.
Cimarron, N.M.

Sirs:
    Enclosed herewith please find check No. 190 - of this date on U.S. Depository at this place, to order of Wellbourne and Stockton for $970.00 being amount due for Rations delivered to Capt. W. P.Wilers, U.S.A., Agent for Utes and Apache Indians, at Cimarron N.M. Sept 30 - Oct 10, and 20.
Please acknowledge receipt, to this office.
              I am very respectfully
              Wm Clinton
              Major U.S.Army
              Supt of Indian Affairs for New Mexico

July 12th
To the Hon.
U.S. District Attorney
For New Mexico
Santa Fe, NM

Sir:
I enclose herewith for your action a list of the names and residences of persons who have been reported to this office as having been engaged in trading whiskey to the Indians of the Cimarron Agency N.M. in violation of the Indian Intercourse Laws, also a list of the names and residences of persons who are said to be able to testify as to the guilt of the accused.
            With much Respect
              Your obedient servant
              Nathanial Pope
              Supt. of Indian Affairs

July 12th 1877
Chas F. Roedel, Esq.
Indian Agent
Cimarron, N.M.

Sir,
Enclose herewith a copy of a letter from Messrs. Wellbourn and Stockton dated Santa Fe N.M. 11th July 1870 declining to feed the Indians at Maxwell's Ranche any longer – their contract having expired June 80th 1870.
    You are authorized to take such steps as you may think necessary to secure the usual supply of provisions to the Indians of your agency at the least possible price per ration.
    You will make arrangements from month to month only, as I have recommended that the Utes and Apaches of your Agency be removed from Cimarron as soon as practical.

Please report your action in the matter of provisions to this office at once.
With much Respect
Your obedient servant
Nathanial Pope
Supt. of Indian Affairs

To
C.F. Roedel, Esq.
Cimarron Agency N.M.

Sir:
I hope to get authentication for my action to remove your Indians from Cimarron and hope you ---these Indians furnish you--- blankets and clothing before the cold weather arrives---have telegraphed to Washington for blankets ---I leave in the morning for Santa Fe to be absent probably 10 days
Respectfully---your obedient servant
Nathanial Pope---Supt of Indians

March 9th 1870
Chas. F. Roedal, Esq
U.S. Indian Agent Cimarron N.M.

Sir
You will please contract and notify the Indians of your Agency that orders have been received from the Bureau of Indian Affairs to remove the Jicarilla Apaches to the Mescalero Apache Agency near Fort Stanton and the Moache Utes to the Abiquiue Agency.
It is desired that their removal from Cimarron should be effected as early as feasible and you will please notify this office how soon in your judgment it can be commenced
        With much respect
        Your obedient servant
        Nathaniel Pope
        Supt. of Indian Affairs

June 22nd
Hon --- E Mix

Sir
    I have been absent from Santa Fe for several days visiting the Cimarron agency for the purpose of assisting the peace commissioners, General Sherman and ---Gappan, and be present at any interview they

might have with the Indians belonging to said agency. The Utes were absent hunting and runners were sent out for them, but as they were so far away, the Commissioners concluded not to remain here until they came in, but postponed the meeting until this fall. The Apaches belonging to this agency are very troublesome at this time. They have been committing a great many depredations lately. They have been stealing sheep, horses, cattle and little children.

      Very Respectfully
      Your Obd-Sevt
      Mr. M Davis
      Clk Indian Dept. N.M.

Hon. --- E. Mix
Act. Commissioner of Indian Affairs
Washington D.C.

Office Supt Indian Affairs
Santa Fe NM July 7th 1868
Maj. E.B. Dennison

Sir
Enclosed herewith I respectfully transmit a special circular from this Department referring to estimates for annuity goods. You will therefore make out, and forward to this office an estimate for goods for next year. Said estimates must be here by August 1st 1868.

Very Respectfully
Your Obt-Svt
Mr. M. Davis
Act. – Supt Indian Affairs New Mexico.

Maj. E.B. Dennison
U.S. Indian Agent
Cimarron N.M.

 Office Supt. Indian Affairs
Santa Fe N.M. Oct 19th 1868
Major R.B. Denison

 Sir
  Your annuity goods will be distributed at the Cimarron Agency Nov 18th 1868 make all necessary arrangements.
I will notify --- --- and have an officer detailed.
 Very Respectfully
 Your Obt-Svt

M. Davis
Ind. Dept. N.M.

Maj. E.B. Dennison

 Sir:
I desire you to be present at my office in Santa Fe NM with six or eight of the principal chiefs of the Moache Utahs of your agency on the 20th of the present month as I have business of importance to transmit.
Very Respectfully
Your Obt Svt
Maj E. B. Dennison
U.S. Indian Agent
Cimarron N.M.

Office Supt Ind Aff
Santa Fe, N.M. Dec 7th 1868
Hon. N.B. Gaylor

 Sir:
Enclosed herewith I have the honor to transmit a communication from Agent G. M. Dodd requesting authority to transmit agriculture implements belonging to the Navajo Indians from Ft. Sumner to Ft Wingate which I approve subject to the approval of the Dept.
Very Respectfully
Your Obt. Servt.
Hon. N.G. Gaylor
Depty Indian Affairs
Washington City D.C.

Office Supt Indian Affairs
Santa Fe N.M. June 7th 1867

Col Tho. N. Dodd

 Sir
   Herewith enclosed find two blank tables for statistics of education, farming which must be reported complete in every item for July 7th 1866 to July 1st 1867. Any items that you are not positive about the amount estimates must be substituted from the best obtainable information. Where there is nothing mark nothing on the blank, but be sure and fill every item. In addition to the above reports you will also make out., your annual report of the condition of the Indians under your charge.

Attend to this matter immediately. So that said reports will be --- at this office before the 10th day of July 1867.

        Very Respectfully your Obt ervant
         A. B. Norton Supt Indian
         Affairs N.M. N.M. Davis
         Clerk

Col. B. N. Dodd
U. S. Indian Agent
A copy of the above letter sent to each of the Agents:
E.B. Dennison Cimarron Agency
Mr. M.M. Harry Abiquiu Agency
Lorenzo Labahada
John Ward Special Agt – Pueblo

Office Supt. Indian Affairs
Santa Fe. N.M. June 23rd 1867

General C. Carson

 Sir
I sent you a bond and oath of office as U.S. Indian Agent for New Mexico on the 8th day of this month. Please inform this office immediately whether you accept said appointment or not.

      Very Respectfully
      Your Obt Servant
       A. B. Norton
      Supt Indian Affairs NM
      M. Davis, Clerk

Genl C. Carson
Ft Garland, Colorado

Office Supt Indian Affairs
Santa Fe NM Aug 20th 1870
  Gen Carson was here last Saturday and still adheres to his determination not to accept of any other agency except that of the Utes & Apaches. I have recommended Mr. Ward to be the full agent for the Pueblo and have no special agents there is one agent and if Judge Sloughs opinion of do good, they should have more. Is Henderson to be paid his salary as he claims up to the time he is replaced by his replacement?
 Many Respects
 A.B. Norton

Hon E. S. Parker
Comm of Indian Affairs for the Ute and Apache Indians
Washington, D.C.

Sir,
I have the honor to transmit herewith a copy of a communication from Mr. C. D. Roedel, Agent for the Ute and Apache Indians dated Cimarron N.M. 17th December 1870 stating that the Indians of his Agency are living on lands owned by an English Company, which company is making strong efforts to sell their lands to actual settlers: that effort in the direction of farming would probably produce meaningful results and also asking to be instructed to receive provisions on the 18th of January 1870.

With the --- intent I wrote to you and suggested that probably starting next year the M. Utes might be persuaded to join the --- and M. Utes of the Abiquiu Agency and that the Jicarilla Apache might be induced to join to the Southern Apache reservation should it be possible. In view of the fact as stated by Agent Roedal I would respectfully recommendat three changes be made as soon as practicable as it proves a savings of expenses to the bureau --- and the Indians will benefit by it.

The contract of misters Willburn and Stockton for feeding the Indians....

February 23st
S. Roedel, Esq.
U. S. Indian Agent
Cimarron, N.M.

Sir:
This office has reason to believe that certain persons about the settlement of Cimarron Agency are engaged in trading whiskey to the Indians of your agency in violation of law.

You will therefore forward to Cimarron --- ostensibly for the purpose of selecting a new location for your agency and ---there you will investigate this matter. Advise with the Cimarron citizens of that place the purpose of ascertaining what persons may be engaged in trading whiskey and also for the purpose of collecting such evidence as will insure the authorities of the guilty parties.

If --- --- beyond a question, the whereabouts of the parties engaged in this unlawful traffic, report to this office at once and I will immediately ask the commanding officer of the District to furnish a detail from Fort Union with an officer to make the arrests.

You are authorized to provide yourself with transportation, with any --- --- that may be missing to make --- --- out this interruption with to fine by this office.

May 31st
Chas S. Roedel
U.S. Indian Agent
Cimarron, NM

Sirs:
You are hereby authorized to continue the present contract of Messurs. Wellburn and Stockton for feeding the Indians of your Agency during the month of June 1870
   With much Respect
   Your obedient servant
   Nathaniel Pope
Supt. of Indian Affairs
By Daniel Catanach, Clerk

Office Superintendant of Indian Affairs
Santa Fe, New Mexico
December 12, 1868

Hon N.F. Taylor
Commissioner of Indian Affairs
Washington, D.C.

Sir,
Owing to the particular state in which I find the several tribes of Indians in this Superintendancy I have the honor now to submit at their request the following items for your information concerning the Utes and Apaches of the Abiquiu and Cimarron Agencies as from such information as I have been able to get from previous source, there is a great misunderstanding as to the status and condition of these tribes.
   The Utes proper of my Superintendency number from two thousand and eight hundred to three thousand, these Indians are quiet and peaceable committing no depredations whatever that have been reported to their agents, the only person to whom such reports should be made, they inform me that they have heard from Mr. Arny and others that the government expects them to go on a Reservation in Colorado Territory in accordance with a treaty which some designing persons have made the Senate of the United States believe they (the Indians) are cognizant of

and that their chiefs signed, when in fact they know nothing of the matter, and they wish me (and I feel it my duty.) to set them right before the department and the Senate.

How the facts are that the parties empowered to make the last treaty with the Utes sought and obtained the consensus of a Capote Indian called Caronnilla, a notorious thief and renegade who signed the treaty with a different name (Oh bu Sah) and two chiefs of the Moache tribe named Hanaishe and Anhalost neither of whom as I am assured by the tribes themselves had authority or power to sign a treaty or power to sign a treaty for them and whose action in doing as they justly declare can never find them in any respect.

I have therefore called the chiefs of the Utes of this Superintendancy to meet me here at Santa Fe on the 20th inst then and there to enable me to ascertain with certainty the wishes of those tribes and defiantly to report the same to you. I do honestly request and hope that you will at once stop all action on the supposed treaty referred to until you receive my report as a misunderstanding might cause a costly war with a powerful tribe of Indians who are now at peace and friendly to the government and who desire to do what is right and proper.

I desire that immediately after such council shall have been held that each of the tribes represented therein shall themselves select say two of their number who shall be their representative men fully authorized and empowered to act in all matters for the tribe and of my action shall meet the approbation of the Department I would here respectfully ask that I may be authorized to bring such representatives on to Washington, that their wishes, wants and needs to this may be fully understood.

                I have the honor to be
                Very respectfully
                Your obt. Svnt
                T Gallegos
                Supt Indian Affairs NM

Office Supt of Indian Affairs
Santa Fe NM Dec 15th 1868
U.S. Special Agent

Sir:
You are hereby ordered to proceed immediately to the Cimarron agency and with unnecessary delay bring to this office six or eight of the principal men belonging to the Mowache tribe of Utahs of said agency. I have very important business to transact with said Indians and you must not fail to have them in Santa Fe as soon as convenient.

                Very Respectfully
                Your obt Servant
                T Gallegos
                Supt of Indian Affairs Terty NM

Capt J M S of Baca
US Special Indian Agent

Office Supt of Indian Affairs
Santa Fe NM Dec 16 1868
L. B. Maxwell, Esq.

Dear Sir.
    As it is necessary for the salvation of the Indians and people of the northern part of the Territory that this treaty which I enclosed should be exposed and set in a brite light before the Senate of the U.S. I wish you to try and have the chiefs of the Utes meet me here at Santa Fe, that I may hold a council with them here so as to represent their true wishes as Supt. of the Ind. Depart. of this Territory. I wrote you this letter myself and will feel indebted you if you will answer me individually as soon as possible, as there is so many men in company as I understand with this --- that of course it becomes me to trust no one with this matter but yourself in the absence of Maj. Dennison from the Agency.
    Knowing that you will take a deep interest in this matter and understand my position it will be not necessary for me to say any more.
I am very respectfully
Your obd Servt
J Gallegos
Sept. of Indian Affairs
Terty of NM

Office Supt of Indian Affairs
Territory of New Mexico
Santa Fe NM Dec 28 1868
Major E. B. Dennison
US Indian Agent for Mouaches Indians

Major,
    I very much desire from you at the earliest possible moment a report of the status of the Indians under your charge, you will see the urgent necessity of this by the present developments of a treaty said to have been made and concluded between representatives of the government and the Utes of your agency which provides for their removal to Colorado, and which in my opinion is contrary to their wishes.
Very respectfully your obedient servant,
T Gallegos
Supt of Indian Affairs

Office Supt. of Indian Affairs
Territy of New Mexico
Santa Fe NM Dec 30 1868

Hon N.G. Taylor
Comm Indian Affairs
Washington DC

Sir
I have the honor to transmit the following Special Reports pertaining to be Indians under the supervision of this Superintendancy.
Special report from this office
    "   " of Capote and Comentata Utah Indians
    "   " Utah and Apache of the Cimarron
    "   " Mescalero Apache
    Mimbres and Mogollin Apuaho
    Pueblo Indians (Agent Quintana)
    Pueblo Indians (Agent Ward)
With hopes that these reports will receive due attentation.
    I am Serv very respectfully
    Your obedient servant
    I Gallegos
      Supt of Indian Affairs
        Terty of NM

Office Supt of Indian Affairs
Santa Fe, NM March 3rd 1869
Vicente-Romero
La Cueva, NM
Dear Sir,
    I enclose herewith a letter from Agt EB Dennison relative to depredations committed against you by the Ute Indians and making the following inquires viz 1. Did the Indians, who committed these depredations belong to the Mohaucha Utes or Jicarilla Apaches, for which he is agent – (Cimarron Agency) 2d at what place were these depredations committed.
    Please answer these questions and return the enclosed letter together with your answer to this office.
        I am very respectfully
        Your obedient servant
        T. --- Gallegos
        Supt. of Indian Affairs for New Mexico

Office Supt. of Indian Affairs
Santa Fe NM August 1st 1869
Bvt-Captain ASB Keyes, USA
U.S. Indian Agent Present

Captain,
   You will proceed without delay to Cimarron, NM, and relieve S.B.Dennison, Esq, US Indian agent, at that place who will be directed to turn over to you all public property, moneys etc in his possession belonging to the agency taking your receipt therefore, instructions relative to your duties will be given you from time to time by this office.
   Owing to the accidental death of Lieut. J,J. Ennis, 3rd Calvy Comay for Indians at Cimarron. You will in addition to your other duties, act as Comay at your agency and will report to Bvt Captain Chas. M. Cline, Chf. Comay , Dept of NM for orders and instruction relative to these duties.

I am very respectfully
Your obedient servant
W Clinton
Major USA Supt of Indian
Affairs for New Mexico

Office Supt. of Indian Affairs
Santa Fe NM August 18 1869
Hon E.S. Parker
Commer. Indian Affairs
Washington, D.C.
Sir
   I have the honor to enclose estimates for the year ending June 30th 1871 for the different tribes of Indians composing this Superintendancy. Owing to the short time I have been in this section of country, (since July 31st) and the fact that but three agents have as yet arrived at their agencies, Lieuts. Cooper and Ford agents for the Pueblos, and Lt. Hanson Agent for the Capoto and Wemenuloha Utes at Abiqiuu. I am unable to submit perhaps as correct estimates as could have been done, had the time been longer on the other agents at these posts. The estimates were all made out at this place from the best information we could get, Capt. F.A. Bennett, Agent for the Navajos started for his post on the 16th inst. in company with Bvt Maj. General Getty and Bvt. Lt Col. Carey, Paymaster who goes to pay the troops in that vicinity.
   Lieut. A.G. Hennssee, Agent for the Mescalero Apache started the same day Fort Stanton with instructions to try and have a talk with those Indians.
   Bvt Capt ASB Keyes, Agent for the Utes and Apaches at Cimarron, started the same day for that place.
   Lieut. C.E. Drews, has not yet reported at this office.
   As a means of saving expenses at the same time to prevent mistakes I would respectfully recommend that the articles intended for the different agents be forwarded direct to them at their agencies as I think that contracts can be made to deliver at the different agencies on better terms

than can be done if the goods are all delivered at this his agency place and new contracts entered into.

No estimate is made for the Navajos as Capt. Bennett had no means of knowing what amount of goods was on hand at his agency and he had instruction from Washington to have a talk with the Navajos and ascertain what articles they most stood in need of.

I am very respectfully your obt servant
W. Clinton
Maj. U.S.Army
Dept. of Indian Aff Affairs

Office Supt. of Indian Affairs
Santa Fe NM Sept 18th 1869
Bvt Capt ASB Keyes USA
Indian Agent
Cimarron, New Mexico

Sir:

I have the honor to acknowledge the receipt of your estimate of funds for part of the 8th and for the 1st--- Quarter 1869 and also your letter of transmittal accompanying the same. I think some of your conclusions are erroneous particularly in which you say that you have estimated your expenses for house rent at what would be your compensation as an officer of the army. I have written to the Adjutant General of the Army in relation to this matter and he has informed me that as soon as a decision had been arrived ay I would be informed.

I send you check for $800. Please sign the enclosed receipt and return them to
Your obedient servant
Wm Clinton
Major US Army
Supt. of Indian Affairs for New Mexico

Office Supt of Indian Affairs
Santa Fe NM Nov 11th 1869

Bvt Capt ASB Keyes, USA
Indian Agent. Cimarron NM

Sir

I have the honor to acknowledge the receipt of your report for October 1869 in which you request me to furnish blankets for your Indians and permission to trade certain articles.

Had you complied with the requirements of my communication to you of Sept 1st – instead of asking in reply- You could have had the required number of blankets forwarded to you with the other goods, at present I can find no transportation for the blankets, besides you do not give the number required. You will ascertain, and report to me, if blankets can be purchased at or near your agency and if so at what prices.
   I cannot give permission to trade on article for another
     I am very respectfully
     Your obedient servant
     Wm Clinton
     Major USA Supt. of Indian Affairs for New Mexico

Office Supt. of Indian Affairs
Santa Fe NM December 4th 1869

Hon E.S. Parker
Comm. of Indian Affairs
Washington, D.C.

Sir,
   I have the honor to acknowledge the receipt of your communication of the 23rd ulta in which you inform me that the contract by me with L.B. Maxwell for furnishing rations for the Indians of the Cimarron Agency was approved (the contract was made with Wellbourn and Stockton and not with L.B. Maxwell)
   You also inform me in the same letter that as the Mohauhe, Capote and other bands of the Utes are parties to a treaty with some of bands of the tribe or nation by which they agree to settle in the southern portion of Colorado that it is not the intention of the Department to furnish supplies to the Indians, except the reservation provided for them. The condition you mention leaves me in some doubt how to act in the matter, as you will perceive that the supplies contract for are to be delivered at the Cimarron, and I do not think the contracts would be written to deliver them at any other place. I would however respectfully draw your to the Report on Indian Affairs by the acting Commissioners for the year of 1867 by which you will see that the Mouach Utes number --- --- and the Jicarilla Apaches --- by which it appears that the Utes are only a little more than one third of the Indians at the Cimarron. As I am not aware of the Apaches being bound by any treaty I do not presume it is the intention of the department to ship the supplies. I shall however await a seasonable time say --- about Christmas before telegraphing the contracts that the contract has been approved at the same time it should relieve me from a great deal of --- and greatly facilitate matters if I should relieve me from a great deal of worry and greatly facilitate

matters if I should receive instructions by telegraph, as the contractors commerce delivering supplies on the 1st of January 1870.

I regard to the Capote and Wamantohes I enclose you the proceedings of an interview held with them in Santa Fe in the 28th of December 1868 which probably shows their feelings as well if not better than anything that can be ascertained at present as these Indians are now out on the hunt.

I will however get the reports of Lomito Hanson, and Capt. Keyes as soon as possible and immediately forward them to the Department.

I will further state that supplies in the way of foods, clothing, powder, and lead are being issued to the Indians at the time I took charge of this superintendancy and suffering it was all proper --- and --- were being issued to these Indians at time I took charge of the superintendancy and supposing it was all proper. I have continued the plan. Their supplies will be exhausted at the end of this month and then should it be the intention of the Department not to furnish any more no other contracts need to be made, such a course I must in frankness state would be made, such a course I must in frankness state stop would in my opinion could cost the government and the people of the territory a large amount of money.

The Capote and Mouncha Indians have the reputation of being the bravest and at the same time the best behaved Indians in the Territory. Of one thing I am fully convinced and that is they cannot be removed from there present homes by forces, nor do I think the Moache can be either.

For the reasons given I think it should be to the advantage of the Government to supply the wants of these Indians for a short time longer, or until another path can be had with them and if so I would respectfully ask on this case also, that I be informed by telegraph.

I am very respectfully
Your obedient servant
Wm Clinton
Major US Army
Supt. of Indian Affairs for New Mexico

                                      Office Supt of Indian Affairs
                                      Santa F. N.M. Jany. 24, 1870

Bvt Capt. A.S. B. Keyes, USA
Agent for Ute and Apache Indians
                Cimarron NM
Sir

I have been waiting for some time to hear from the Bureau in relation to feeding and supplying your Indians, and received a letter in reply thereto this morning but as it contains nothing satisfactory. I am still at a loss to know how to ask, however as the contract for rations has been approved, you can go on and find that Indians under that contract, but as I do not wish the contracts to labor under my false impression that the Indians will remain where they are. You will inform them that it is my impression that the Indians will be removed as soon I cannot tell, but I think in the spring.

Gen. McCook, Supt for Colorado, has been directed to visit me at Santa Fe and then he and I will visit your agency and also the agency of the --- to see what was to be done. In the mean time you will on every occasion impression upon the Indians the advantage it --- to be --- to comply with the wishes of the government and go on the reservation laid out for them.

In am very respectfully
Your obedient servant
Wm Clinton
Major USA Supt of Indian Affairs
for NM

Office Supt. of Indian Affairs
Santa Fe N.M.
Feby 7, 1870

Bvt Capt. A.S.B. Keyes, U.S.A.
Agent for Ute and Apache Indians,
Cimarron N.M.

Sir:

I have the honor to acknowledge the receipt of your communication of the inst and in reply would state that as the contract has been approved, I do not think that the accounts will be disallowed however you should be able to judge of that as well as myself one thing is certain the Indians are there and I do not think it is the intention of the Government to share this until such time as measures are taken to transport them to their new homes.

My reasons for directing you to discontinuing feeding the Utes was that I had neither heard from the Bureau nor Gen. McCook, and I did not feel warrants in feeding them any longer is my own responsibility. You can make out the forms to see for your self

I am very respectfully
Your obedient servant
W. Clinton
Major U.S. Army

Supt. of Indian Affairs for NM

Office Supt of Indian Affairs
Santa Fe NM
Feby 10 1870

Bvt. Capt. A.S. B. Keyes U.S.A.
Cimarron, New Mexico

Sir:
    In a letter dated Denver, Feb. 1 1870, Gen. McCloud says, owning to the fact the Territorial Legislature is in session, it will be impossible for me to comply with the request (meeting the Utes in New Mexico) at present I want to inform you in order that you may communicate the informalities to the Indians that ample provisions has been made for their support on the reservations.
    There are means at the Ute Agency in charge of Lieut. Spear, U.S.A. 100,000 pounds of wheat and flour of sugar 10 bails (bales) of blankets, clothing and other annuity goods of various description.
    You will make that known to your Indians and tell them that as requested by Gen. McCloud and have ----- he and I will visit them for the purpose of having a talk and knowing what the Indians have to say.

        I am very respectfully
        Your obedient servant
        W. Clinton
        Major U.S. Army
        Supt. of Indian Affairs for New Mexico

Office Supt. of Indian Affairs
Santa Fe NM February 10 1870

--- --- Edward M. McCloud
--- Office Supt. of Indian Affairs
Denver, Colorado
Sir:
    I have the honor to acknowledge the receipt of your communication of the 4th, informing me that on account of the Legislature being in session you cannot visit New Mexico at this time, I am very sorry for them as in the spring the streams are as high as to render it very difficult traveling in the San Juan Country where the most of the Utes are located. It is also very –desirable that the Indians should understand the limitations of the Government as now very much is In a state of uncertainty. I do not know myself whether to find --- or not , as long as they are being fed where the here they will show no difficulty on the reservation, and to stop feeding them without some understanding

would. I have no doubt --- to --- that would eventually --- to ---. You will therefore see the importance of our continue places visit bring made as early a date as possible.

You speak of meeting me at the Cimarron, would it not be better for you to give thought to Santa Fe and there we might go to the San Juan Country first where it is about --- Indians where there were but about --- at the Cimarron. You would also inform the agent (as you pass through) at about the time we could be there and in the --- he would gather his Indians together.

Should you however decide to visit the Cimarron first if you will inform me in time I will meet you there.

I shall send extracts for your letter to the agents in charge of the Utes, at the same time it is as well to inform you that I have written --- the agents to impress, at all times upon the Indians the advantages it --- to be them, to go on the reservation.

                I am very respectfully
                Your obedient servant
                Wm Clinton

Major US Army (visiting the Utes in New Mexico) at present --- I want to inform you in order that you may communicate the information to the Indians that --- --- --- month for their support on the reservations.

        --- --- --- at the --- Ute agency in charge of Lieut. Spears USA --- --- --- -- --- 10 bales of blankets, clothing and other annuity goods of --- --- sends information.

You will make this known to your Indians and tell them that --- --- --- Gen. McCloud can have blankets he and I will visit them for the purpose of having a talk and knowing what the Indians have to say.

                I am very respectfully
                Your obedient servant
                Wm Clinton
                Major US Army
                Super of Indian Affairs for New Mexico

Office Supt. of Indian Affairs
Santa Fe NM April 9th 1870

Hon. SB Parker
Commissioner of Indian Affairs
Washington, D.C.

      Sir:

In order that I may have time to advertise for supplies for the use of the agencies attached to this Superintendancy for the six months ending Dec 31st 1870 I would respectfully ask that I be informed of about the probable amount of funds that will be furnished for that period.

By a reference to my request of Dept 20th of 1869 it will be seen that the following sums have been asked for viz:

Navajoes for annuity goods in accordance with Article 8 treaty of June 1^s 1868

$60,000.00 For seeds, agriculture implements, etc.
 20,000.00 For completing agency buildings
 20,000.00 For feeding those who are in need
 40,000.00 For corn, hay, fuel, stabling
Total for Navajoes   144,000.00

Capote and Mohaucha Utes, at Aliqie, New Mexico for provisions $12,000.00
For rent of agency, --- --- for stabling
3,000.00
For annuity goods
10,000.00
                    Total for Aliqui Agency
20,000.00

Apaches Utes and Jicarilla Apaches at Cimarron NM
For provisions
$18,000.00
For amt agency for hay, fuel, stabling
3,000.00
For annuity goods
10,000.00
Total for Cimarron $30,000.00

Pueblo Indians for establishing schools (including pay of teachers purchasing books building and furnishing school house) $50,000.00
Mescalero Apache for locating on reservation
                                        $5,000.00
For surveying reservation

                                        5,000.00
For subsistence until such time as their --- gathered
                                        30,000.00
For seeds, agriculture implements, work, ---,

Blacksmith and carpenters tools
10,000.00
For annuity goods
5,000.00
For building storehouse, corrals, agents houses, workshops   8,000.00
For hay, corn, fuel, stationary, etc
2,000.00
Total for Mescalero Apaches
65,000.00

Mimbries and Mogollon Apache for locating on reservations $5,000.00
For surveying reservation
5,000.00
For subsisting them until their crops are gathered
45,000.00
For seeds, agriculture implements, work cattle, blacksmiths
And carpenters tools etc
15,000.00
For annuity goods
16,000.00
For buildings, storehouses, corrals, agents houses, workhouses etc   80,000.00
For hay, corn, fuel, stabling, etc
3,000.00
Total for southern Apache agency
90,000.00
Superintendancy, rent of building
$600.00
For clerk hire
1,500.00
For hire of porter and teamster
960.00
For corn, hay, stabling
3,000.00
Total for Superintendancy
6,000.00
Total required for the Territory
405,000.00
For hire of eight Interpreters, at $300 per annum
4,000.00   In order that I may not fall into the error I did last Fall of contracting for more than I had money to pay for. I would sure respectfully request that I be directed to advertise for

such articles as the Department may allow to the different tribes.

I think it would be advantageous for the Department to advertise ay once for any farming implements they expect to give the Indians, so that they may be delivers this fall and ready for use in this spring.

The difficulty I am laboring under at present is the implements --- purchased have to be brought from the states this spring and as a arrangement causes great delay in planting.

I am very respectfully
W. Clinton
Major USA

Authors note:

In reading the above letters, the author has compiled the following lists:

Superintendants of Indian Affairs, Santa Fe New Mexico:
- Clinton
- Pope
- Delgado
- Norton
- Mix
- Galegos
- Collins

Commissioners of Indian Affairs Washington D.C.:
- Parker
- Wm. P. Dole
- Dennis Cooley
- Lewis V. Bogy
- Nathaniel G. Taylor

Indian Agents in Cimarron, NM:
- Levi J. Keithly 1862
- Alexander G. Irvine 1864
- Manuel S. Salazar 1865
- Erasmus B. Dennison 1866
- Lt. A. S. B. Keyes 1869
- Maj. W. P. Wilson 1870
- Charles E. Roedel 1870
- John E. Pyle 1875
- (source: FamilySearch.org)

Special Agent: Baca

15. Bibliography

Chase Orchard: A Poñil Phase Pueblo in the
Cimarron District,
Northeastern New Mexico
By James A. Gunnerson
Memoir 11 of the Oklahoma Anthropological Society
Robert E. Bell Monographs in Anthropology 4 of the
Sam Nobel Oklahoma Museum of Natural History
2007

Lucien Bonaparte Maxwell
Napoleon of the Southwest
By Lawrence R. Murphy

Out in God's Country: A History of Colfax County,
New Mexico
By Larry Murphy

For Good or Bad
People of Cimarron Country
Compiled and Edited by Stephen Zimmer

Lucien Maxwell
Villain or Visionary
By Harriet Freiberger

Introduction to Early American Masonry
Stone, Brick, Mortar and Plaster
By Harley J. McKee, F.A.I.A.
Published by National Trust for Historic Preservation
and Columbia University

Figure 1: Portrait of Lucien Bonaparte Maxwell.

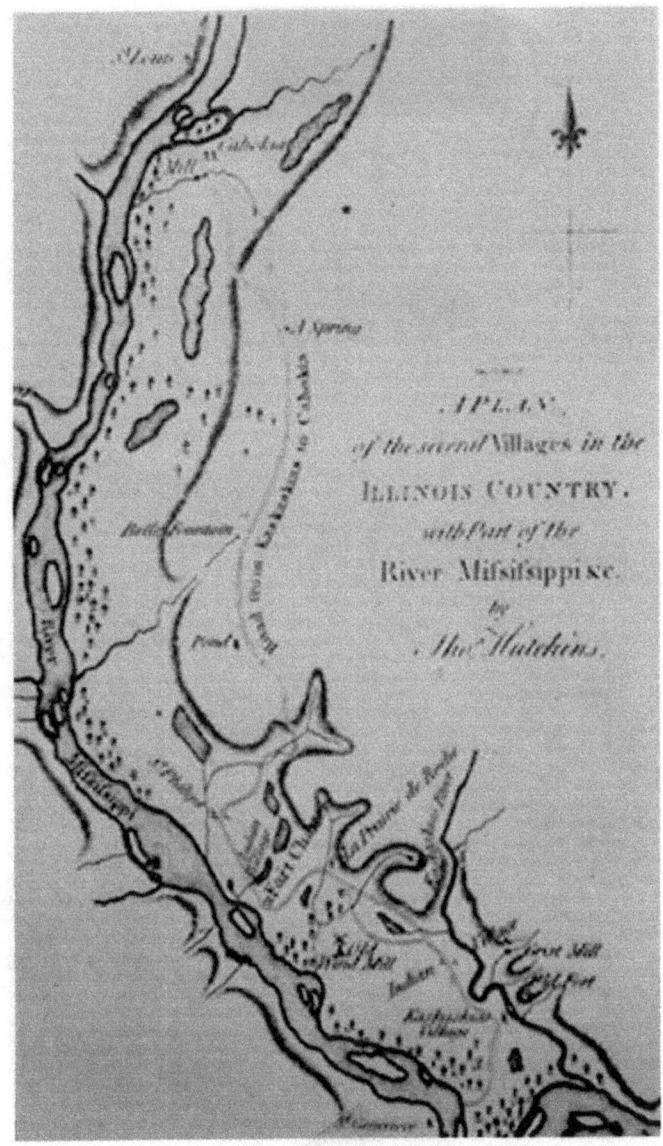

Map by Thomas Hutchins, 1771

Figure 2: Map showing Illinois Country where Lucien grew up and location of three grist mills drawn by Thomas Hutchins in 1771.

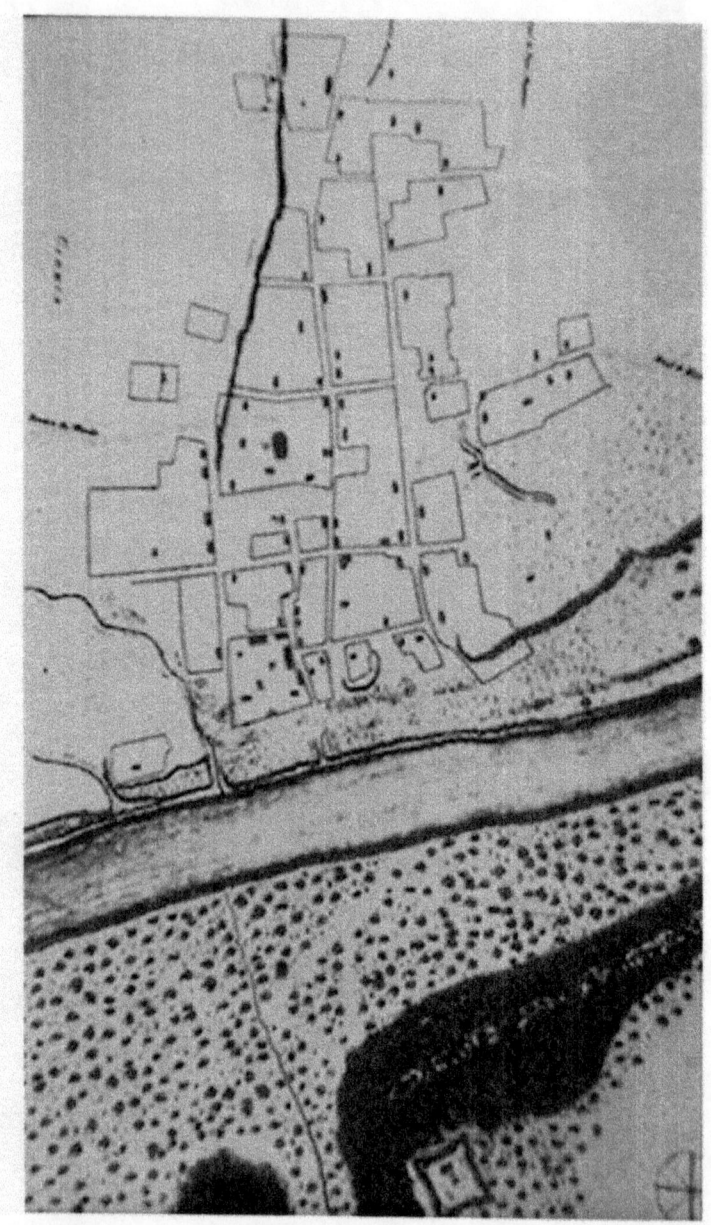

Figure 3: Map of Kaskaskia drawn by Thomas Hutchins in 1766 shows town roads, buildings, Mississippi River and Kaskaskia River.

Figure 4: Summarized map of Illinois Country as printed in the *Historical Atlas of Canada*, 1987 showing roads, French settlement, Indian settlements, mills, and rivers.

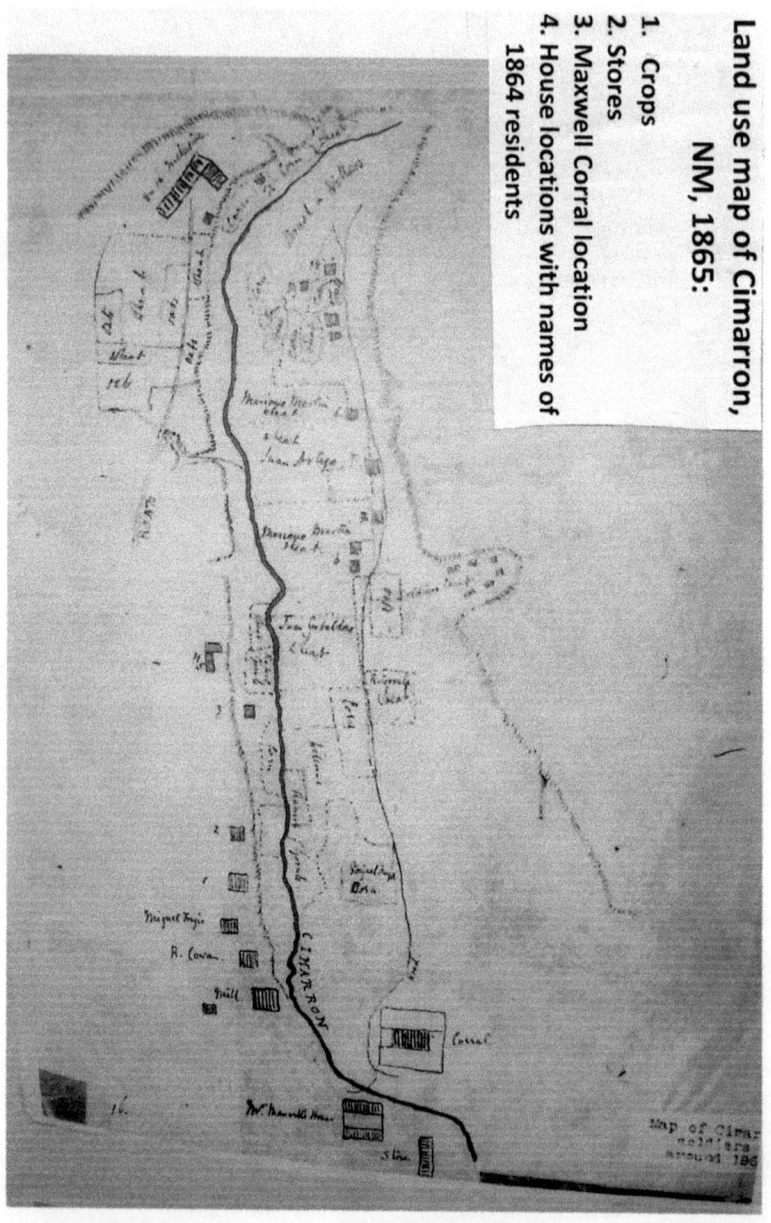

Figure 5: Map of Cimarron 1865 shows early buildings (Maxwell's corral, Maxwell house, store, mill) and residences with cultivated plots and crops grown.

Figure 6: Pierre Menard House is a historic house once occupied by Lucien's grandfather. Built in early 1800s of vertical logs.

Figure 7: Creole House that is very similar to the house of Lucien Maxwell shown in Maxwell's Ranche photograph. House was built in 1801 and is located Prairie du Rocher, Illinois.

The main gate at Fort de Chartres as reconstructed for the state park.

Figure 8: Masonry of main gate at Fort de Chartes located at Kaskaskia.

The stone powder magazine is the only Fort de Chartres structure that has survived from the French period. This picture of the restored building was made by the author in 1965.

Figure 9: Powder magazine begun in 1753 is the oldest surviving non-Indian structure in the Midwest. A masonry building in scope and size to Aztec Mill in Cimarron built by Lucien Maxwell.

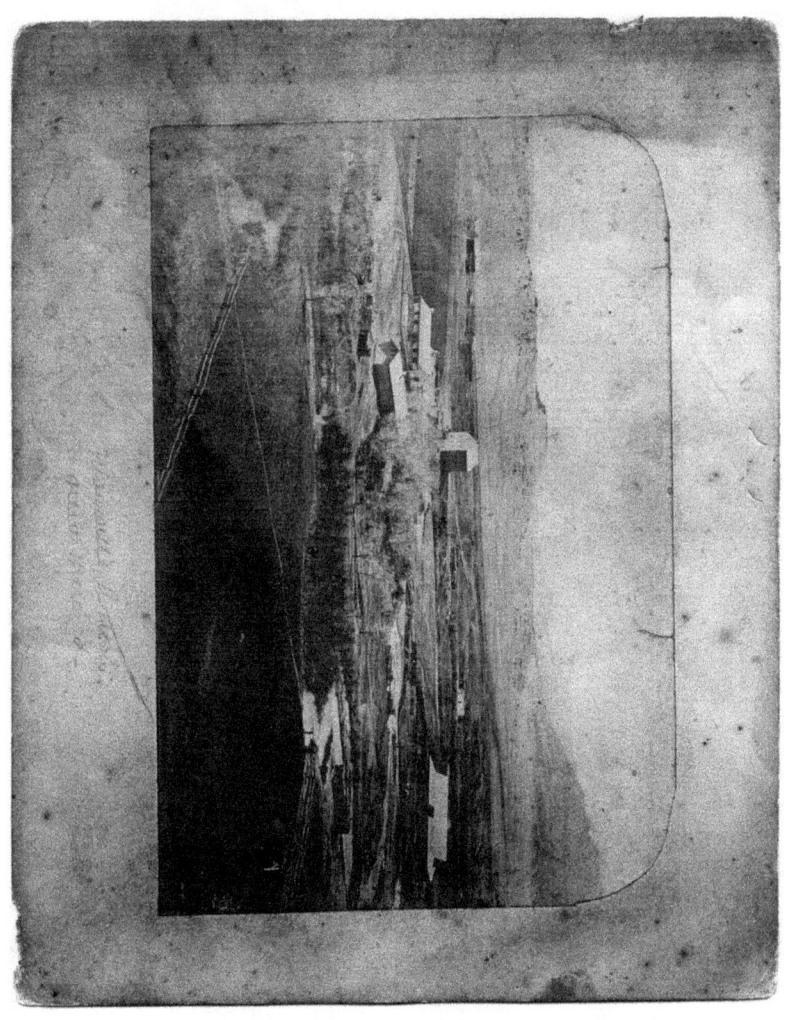

Figure 10: Maxwell's Ranche photograph. This wide angle view is the earliest photo of settlement that would become Cimarron, NM and surrounding environs.

Figure 11: Close up view of Maxwell's Wagon yard showing Aztec Mill, Maxwell's houses, trading post/store and log structures.

Figure 12: Extreme close up view of Maxwell's wagon yard showing: wagon, two log buildings, two sets of wagon wheels and reduced images of groups of mounted riders.

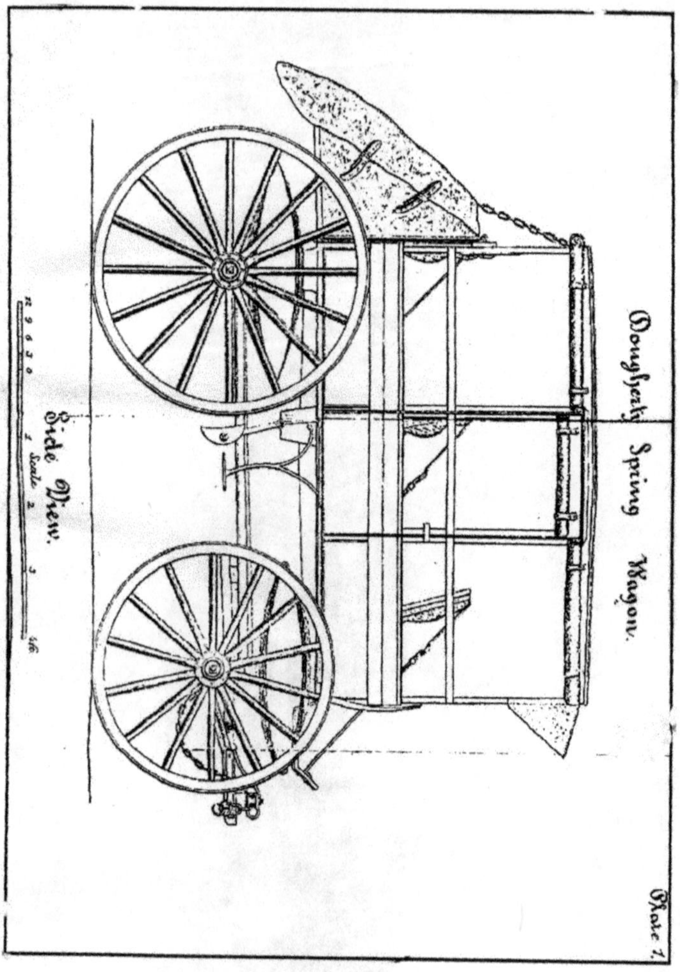

8.9. Dougherty spring wagon as illustrated in *Specifications for Means of Transportation*, 1882. Courtesy of the U.S. Army Quartermaster Museum.)

Figure 13: Doughtery Spring Wagon 1882.

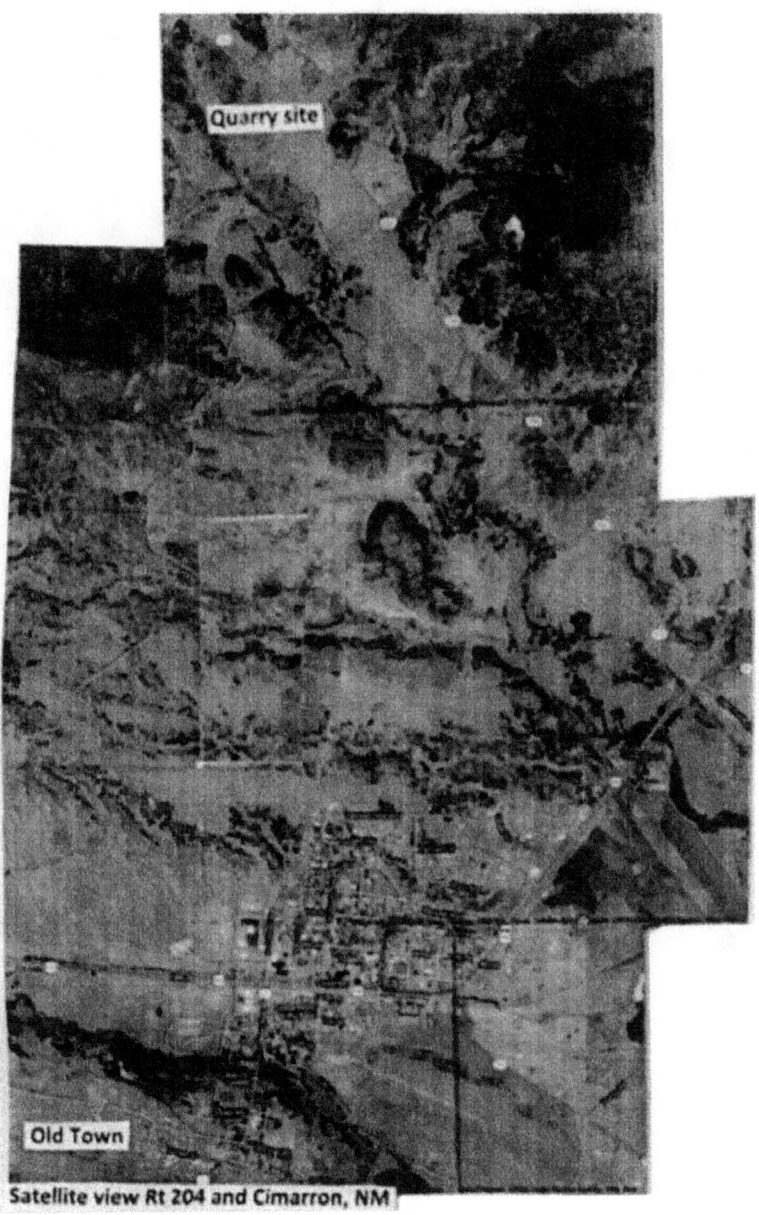

Figure 14: Satellite view of source of mill sandstone with transport routes to Cimarron.

Figure 15: View of location of quarry from NM Route 204.

Figure 16: Quarry site photograph taken from NM Route 204.

Figure 17: Close up of quarry site work surfaces. Photo taken from NM Route 204.

Figure 18: Aztec Mill masonry detail showing sandstone blocks used in Mill construction.

Figure 19: Cimarron River flood plain today, site of Maxwell's corral.

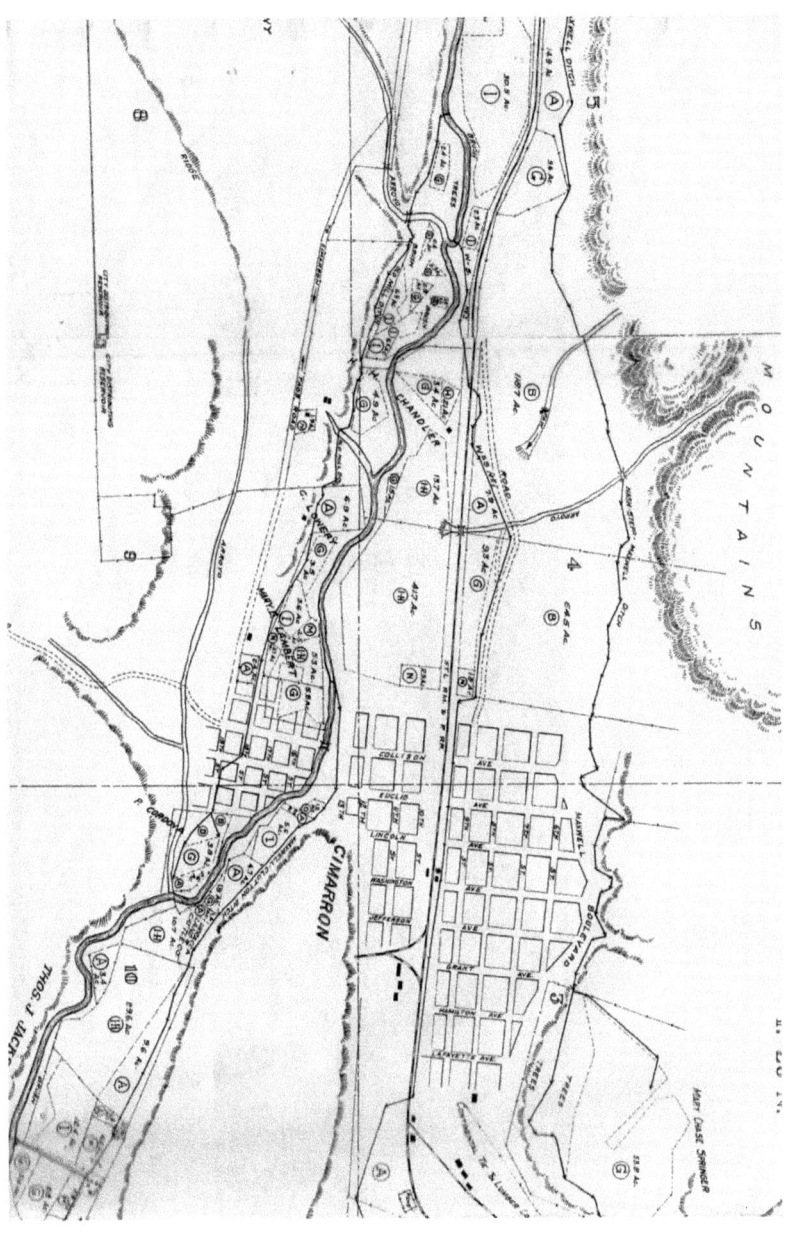

Figure 20: Source of mill water map drawn by Cimarron Hydrographic Survey 1923.

Figure 21: Building foundation as drawn by Oliver Evans, published in *The Young Mill-Wright and Millers Guide 1798*.

Figure 22: Construction scaffolding. The author points out this sketch of stone work, iron work and scaffolding is adapted to Aztec Mill, Cimarron, NM from a drawing in *Mill* by David Macaulay, published by Houghton Mifflin Company of Boston, MA in 1983.

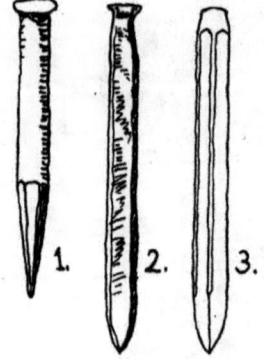

POINTS.
1. Type used since ancient Roman times.
2. Italian, 16th century.
3. American, 19th century.

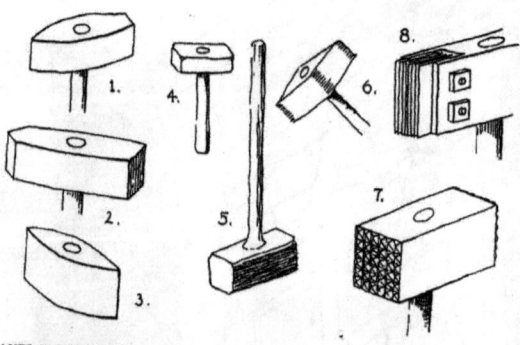

AXES AND HAMMERS.
1. Face hammer.
2. Face hammer; 8 inches long, 2½ inch cutting edge. Mercer Museum, Doylestown, Pa.
3. Ax or pean-hammer; 5¼ inches long, 3 inch cutting edge. Mercer Museum.
4. Hand hammer.
5. Sledgehammer.
6. Ax or pean-hammer.
7. Bush hammer.
8. Patent hammer.

Figure 23: Mill masonry construction tools have changed little since the advent of steel.

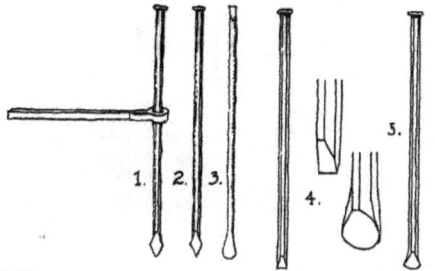

DRILLS.
1. 19th century.
2. 19th century.
3. Italian, 16th century.
4. 23 inches long, 1 inch octagonal. Mercer Museum, Doylestown, Pa.
5. 31½ inches long, 1 inch octagonal, 1¼ inch cutting edge. Mercer Museum.

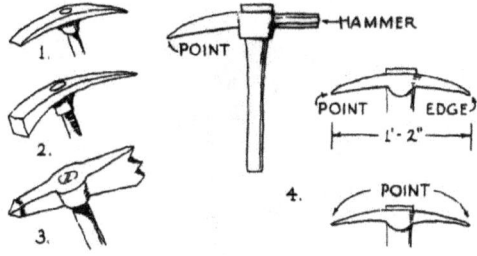

PICKS.
1. Mason's pick with chisel end.
2. Hammer-headed or pole pick.
3. Italian, 16th century.
4. Picks, Mercer Museum, Doylestown, Pa.

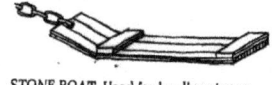

STONE BOAT. Used for hauling stones.

Figure 24: Mill masonry construction tools.

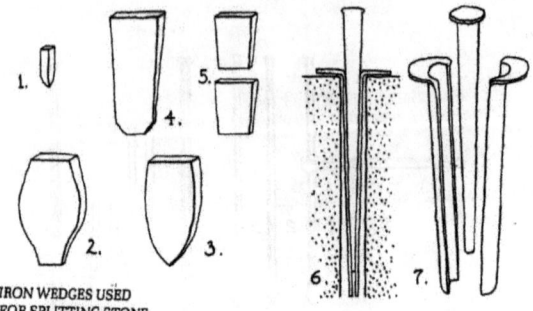

IRON WEDGES USED
FOR SPLITTING STONE.

1. 2¼ inches long, ½ inch square.
Mercer Museum, Doylestown, Pa.
2-3. Flat wedges.

4-5. Modern English wedges with slats.
6. Square plug and feathers.
7. Round plug and feathers.

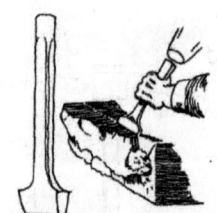

PITCHING CHISELS. American, 19th century. Pitching chisels have a flat face instead of a cutting edge.

Figure 25: Mill masonry construction tools.

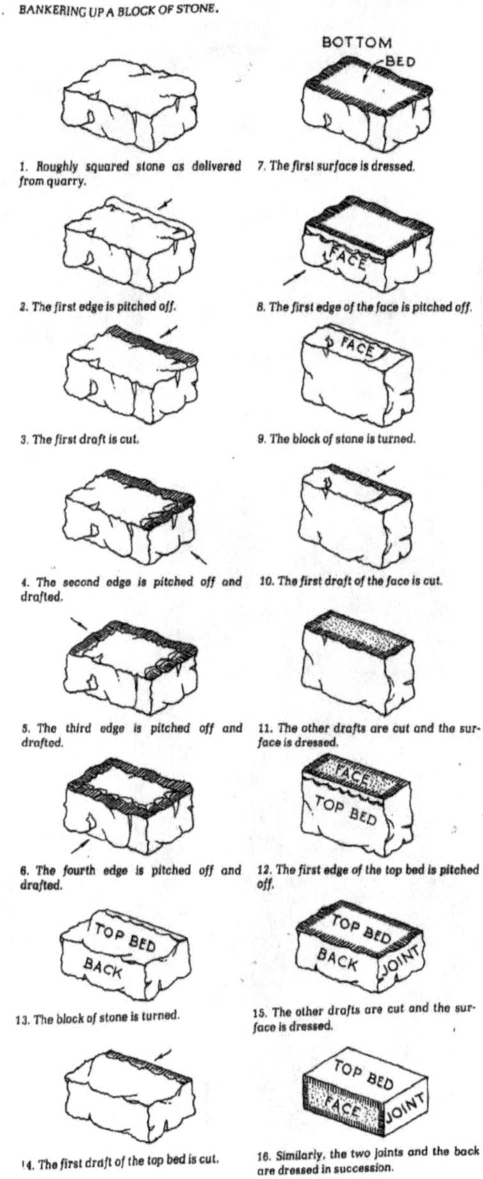

BANKERING UP A BLOCK OF STONE.

1. Roughly squared stone as delivered from quarry.

2. The first edge is pitched off.

3. The first draft is cut.

4. The second edge is pitched off and drafted.

5. The third edge is pitched off and drafted.

6. The fourth edge is pitched off and drafted.

7. The first surface is dressed.

8. The first edge of the face is pitched off.

9. The block of stone is turned.

10. The first draft of the face is cut.

11. The other drafts are cut and the surface is dressed.

12. The first edge of the top bed is pitched off.

13. The block of stone is turned.

14. The first draft of the top bed is cut.

15. The other drafts are cut and the surface is dressed.

16. Similarly, the two joints and the back are dressed in succession.

Figure 26: Diagram: Bankering up a Block of Stone.

Figure 27: Aztec Mill on ration day 1868.

MAXWELL GRIST MILL AT CIMARRON

Figure 28: Aztec Mill back view.

www.ingramcontent.com/pod-product-compliance
Lightning Source LLC
Chambersburg PA
CBHW070100100426
42743CB00012B/2605